Just-In-Time for Today and Tomorrow

Just-In-Time for Today and Tomorrow

▼

Taiichi Ohno
with
Setsuo Mito

Translated by
Joseph P. Schmelzeis, Jr.

Foreword by
Norman Bodek, President
Productivity, Inc.

Productivity Press
Cambridge, Massachusetts and Norwalk, Connecticut

Originally published as *Naze hitsuyō na mono wo hitsuyō na bun dake hitsuyō na toki ni teikyō shinainoka? — Toyota seisan hooshiki kara keiei shisutemu e*

Additional copies of this book are available from the publisher.
Address all inquiries to:

Productivity Press, Inc.
P.O. Box 3007
Cambridge, Massachusetts 02140
United States of America
(617) 497 – 5146

Library of Congress Catalog Card Number: 88-42624
ISBN: 0-915299-20-8

Cover and book design by Stanton Design, Cambridge, Massachusetts
Typeset by Rudra Press, Cambridge, Massachusetts
Printed and bound by Maple-Vail Book Manufacturing Group
Printed in the United States of America

Library of Congress Cataloging-in-Publication Data

Ōno, Taiichi, 1912–
Just-in-time for today and tomorrow.

Translation of: *Naze hitsuyō na mono o hitsuyō na bun dake hitsuyō na toki ni teikyō shinai no ka*.
Includes bibliography and index.
1. Just-in-time systems — Japan. I. Mito, Setsuo, 1934– .
II. Title.
TS155.056313 1988 658.5 88-42624
ISBN 0-915299-20-8

88 89 90 91 10 9 8 7 6 5 4 3 2 1

Table of Contents

Publisher's Foreword

Just-In-Time for Today and Tomorrow is the third in our series of books by Taiichi Ohno, esteemed creator of the Toyota production system. It is his most recent work, published in Japan in 1986 as a dialogue and commentary between the Master and his longtime friend Setsuo Mito, well-known business journalist.

If there is one thing we in the manufacturing world have learned in the past decade, it is the importance of the customer. Henry Ford remarked in the 1920s that the customer could have any color Model T — as long as it was black. And that was the name of the game for the next half century. Manufacturers everywhere produced as fast as they could. They made what they thought was best or what the workplace wanted — and the customer selected from what was available.

In the past, when buying a new car, I picked one from the dealer's showroom. I picked from what was available — not necessarily what I preferred in color, accessories, and so on. Otherwise I had to wait ten to 13 weeks to get exactly what I wanted.

Today, according to Mr. Ohno, the marketplace has shifted to being driven by the exact needs and desires of the customer. In Tokyo, at a Toyota showroom, there is no inventory to select from. You see a few models and select colors and options from display catalogs, videos, and computer terminals. In just seven days, a car meeting your exact specifications is ready for you.

A Japanese camera store may offer 1,000 variations from which to choose. Like at a supermarket, you have many different choices. And the manufacturing system must be able to produce exactly what the consumer wants, exactly when the consumer wants it, and in the exact quantity wanted to avoid waste. This is just-in-time production as seen in the marketplace.

Taiichi Ohno is a living treasure of the manufacturing world. Since the 1950s, but particularly following the 1973 oil crisis, he has inspired thousands of operations worldwide — in both production and service industries. He has enabled us to see processes differently. He has taken Ford's mass production system into the future to create a mechanism that works for today's society as well as for tomorrow's.

This book is geared to service industries as well as manufacturers. There are many similarities. Read and find out. You will be amazed at how astute these two men are and how well their ideas apply to our own companies. After all, Mr. Ohno is the first to admit his indebtedness to American concepts such as the Ford system, supermarkets, and most recently, 7-Eleven convenience stores.

Enjoy this very readable book and learn from it. We all can.

For granting us the rights to translate and publish this English edition, I thank Mr. Yuzuma Kawashima, proprietor, and Mr. Katsuyoshi Saito, deputy manager, of Diamond Inc., the Japanese publisher. They have been most helpful to us as a company to make such works available to English readers.

I particularly want to acknowledge Joseph Schmelzeis, this volume's translator, and Cheryl Berling Rosen, its editor, for their devotion to the authors' words and ideas; Esmé McTighe, production manager; Bill Stanton, book and cover designer; the staff of Rudra Press, our typesetters and artists; Steven Ott, general manager; and the entire staff of Productivity Press.

Finally, I wish to express my indebtedness to Taiichi Ohno and Setsuo Mito, the authors, for creating a book that will inspire our readers to further improve the quality and productivity of today's workplace.

Norman Bodek
President
Productivity Inc.

Preface

The Toyota production system is called the just-in-time (JIT) system because it answers the needs of a changing marketplace by providing goods when and in the amounts needed. Looking back at the system's developmental stages, we have witnessed how much individual tastes and values have changed.

The basis of the Toyota production system is the total elimination of waste. Initially, it meant waste surfacing in the manufacturing processes. After trying to identify and eliminate every kind of waste, we concluded that *real* waste was making products that don't sell. Even quality products, if they don't sell, must be discarded. This waste, in fact, is the most crucial because it is not just a loss to the company — it is a loss to society.

We learned something important while examining ways to eliminate waste, both large and small. We learned how abstract the word "public" really is. We discovered that people have individual personalities and that the manufacturing ideal is to make many different products to meet their personal tastes.

It is an illusion to think costs decrease when we manufacture products in large quantities. This illusion, in fact, increases waste and costs. Costs really decrease when goods are produced singly, or in small lots. As long as production was king, the Ford system's mass-producing assembly lines were the most effective.

Today, however, the marketplace rules. In the Toyota system, production starts only when orders arrive from the marketplace or sales department. Nothing begins without this information, which means the information flow is always ahead of the production flow.

This is the management system of today. Thanks to computers and the developing global communication networks, we believe the Toyota production system will go beyond the boundaries of companies, industries, nations, and time.

Taiichi Ohno
Setsuo Mito
February 1988

Preface to the Japanese Edition

Under the various labels of the "kanban system," the "Toyota system," and at times the "just-in-time system," the Toyota production system has become the focus of discussion in many factories and offices. In fact, numerous businesses, regardless of scale or even type of industry, including some in several foreign countries, have implemented this system.

While undergoing this industrial and international expansion, the Toyota production system has undergone a certain kind of evolution. Just as a point can expand to become a line and then a plane, so too has this system evolved into more than just a set of production techniques. It has become a comprehensive management system.

The original concepts behind the Toyota production system were aimed at the entirety — not at a part — of a company's organization. Naturally, therefore, my ambition is to test the Toyota production system as a total management system — across industry boundaries, whether they manufacture goods or handle information — across companies, whether they are as large as Toyota Motors or as small as the local dry cleaner — and indeed across national borders to countries outside Japan. Without repeated and thorough testing under all conceivable conditions, it cannot take root in our society and achieve its goal of totally eliminating waste.

The Toyota production system first attracted attention in Japanese industrial circles after the first oil crisis in the fall of 1973. In that emergency, confronted with zero growth and the necessity for managing with less, many companies fixed their attention on and implemented the Toyota production system with its relentless pursuit of the total elimination of waste. Many criticized this approach and suggested that instead of taking on the challenge represented by such a complete change, it would be better to start with an easier method. To me, this was just an excuse. In rejuvenating a company, there are no easy methods. The extent to which we achieve success is dictated by the degree to which management is committed to innovative change, not making excuses.

The first oil crisis of 1973 changed the tide of Japan's and indeed the world's economic development; not only in the post-war era but into the twenty-first century. Times have changed from the "if we make it, we can sell it" era to the era of material abundance. No longer is it sufficient to produce in ever-increasing quantities — quality and value now are being demanded. Society's values have matured to where a product will not sell if it does not appeal to the various tastes of many different consumers. In today's industrial world, the call is for the production of many kinds in small quantities.

The original concept behind the Toyota production system was the total elimination of waste. Carrying this to its logical conclusion, it follows that the function of industry is to accept orders not from an abstract clump known as "the masses," but from individuals with unique preferences, and to produce unique goods accordingly. Waste and high costs occur when we try to produce similar items in large quantities. It is cheaper by far to produce unique items one by one. The former method is the Ford system — the latter is the Toyota production system.

I do not fault Henry Ford. I think the real problem is in conservative human nature and our unfortunate habit of blindly following authority and relying on strong individuals. I have no intention of denying Henry Ford's incredible effort and creativity. His successors, however, relied too much on the authority of the Ford system.

Another way of stating the essence of the Toyota production system is to say we are doomed to failure if we do not initiate a daily destruction of our various preconceptions. Merging the computer and communications industries will be invaluable in this regard, making it possible to bring together and transmit information essential to the continuous reevaluation of our management systems. Thus, even in our information society rushing on toward the twenty-first century, the basic function and usefulness of the Toyota production system will not change.

In the business world, a trinity is formed by the market, the factory, and the company as a whole. The market tingles at its pulse points with the immediate *Now!* needs of its many unique consumers. The factory takes orders from this market and produces many varieties in small quantities. The company's management strategy fine tunes the factory with the marketplace, grasping precisely the *Now!* needs of the market and reacting instantly. In the factory, this means nothing less than producing goods one at a time in rhythm with the *Now!* information coming from the marketplace.

The Ford system took as its authority forecasts of a necessarily uncertain future based on an analysis of past data and an observation of past trends. This old-fashioned method no longer applies. Advancing toward a high-information society, the Toyota production system demonstrates its value by seizing and giving life to the *Now!* in the company as a management system. The title of this book, *Why Not Do It Just-In-Time?* [The title of the English edition is *Just-In-Time for Today and Tomorrow* — Ed.], expresses what I want most to bring home to today's managers and controllers.

It has been nearly eight years since I first obtained the cooperation of economics journalist Mito Setsuo and published *Toyota Production System: Beyond Large-Scale Production* [English edition (Cambridge, Massachusetts: Productivity Press, 1988)]. Many readers were kind enough to share their invaluable words of advice and criticism. Since then, I have used these ideas gratefully as food for thought and experimentation while walking around factories. For this I wish to express my deep gratitude. During these walks, many new ideas have filled my mind. It also goes without saying that the external environmental changes of the past eight years have been a source of strong and vigorous intellectual stimulation.

As with the earlier book, I have often had the opportunity to use my friend Mito Setsuo as a sounding board for my new ideas and opinions. Mr. Mito, for his part, would always come to my home in Nagoya with new issues to discuss. Our discussions continued this way for over five years. Our talks always started with the Toyota production system but sometimes drifted through time, shifting to the Mikawa locale of the plant and its historical setting for the three great heroes who unified Japan — Ieyusa Tokugawa, Hideyoshi Toyotomi, and Nobunaga Oda.

We also discussed whether, from economic and scientific points of view, the Toyota production system could be transplanted successfully to various foreign countries, despite its strong cultural roots in Japan. The conversations would always end with a discussion of which country would adapt easiest to Toyota's system: Korea, Taiwan, or the United States? And what about China? Starting with the idiosyncratic personality and business of Henry Ford, we often enjoyed discussing various celebrities and the relationship between genius and madness.

When we tired of talking we would go to the factory floor. The factory is a "silent" space that always heightens human awareness and stimulates the imagination. We would return to our room to find our conversation invigorated with new ideas. This book is a collection of topics drawn from those many relaxed and free-flowing conversations, all on the theme of the essence and evolution of the Toyota production system. From beginning to end, I have been able to grapple with these issues while enjoying great freedom of the imagination.

I heartily welcome criticism and comments from our readers.

Taiichi Ohno
February 2, 1986

A Note on Japanese Names

In Japan, the family name appears first. Thus, the famed inventor of the Toyota production system is known in Japan as Ōno Taiichi, and not Taiichi Ohno as usually written in the West.

In this series of Productivity Press books, we try to follow the Japanese practice of placing the surname first. In part, we do this to make the representation of Japanese names uniform, but primarily it is out of common courtesy. The reader therefore will find members of the Toyoda family referred to as Toyoda Sakichi, Toyoda Kiichirō, Toyoda Eiji, and so forth. However, when a person such as Taiichi Ohno is frequently referred to in other publications and the media in the Western manner, we refer to him or her likewise.

Also, when romanizing Japanese characters, a macron is used over a long vowel in all Japanese words except for well-known place names (Kyoto, Tokyo), words that have entered the English language (shogun, daimyo), and individuals' names in which customarily the macron is replaced by an *h* (Ohno, not Ōno).

Just-In-Time for Today and Tomorrow

1

The Management System that Anticipates the Information Age

Theme: Information originates in the market

The fundamental doctrine of the Toyota production system is the total elimination of waste. The two main criteria necessary for achieving that goal are *just-in-time*, or JIT, and *autonomation*, or automation with a human touch.

First, let's pursue the nature of just-in-time. Assume for a moment that a car is being built on an assembly line. JIT occurs when the parts necessary for each step in that process arrive alongside that process at the exact time and in the quantity needed.

Coming up with the JIT system turned the assumptions of history upside down. Humans rarely challenge existing ideas and ways of doing things. Such ideas gain strength and persuasiveness by undergoing the severe tests of time and taking root in society as common sense. Their power is strong indeed.

In the management world and on the production floor, the ideas that described the flow of production can be called *planned mass production*, or the Ford system. Of course, the father of this Ford system is America's Henry Ford (1863–1947) who based his thinking on materials being processed by machines on a conveyor belt. The materials are fashioned into completed parts, whereupon groups of the various parts are provided at a fixed speed to the final assembly line where they are assembled and exit the line. It is a genuine mass production system. The Ford system gave rise to America's "mass production, mass sales" society and naturally took root in postwar Japan when we were challenged to "catch up with America."

It is no wonder, then, that the Toyota production system met with such opposition when it rejected and indeed reversed that "natural" way of doing things. Nevertheless, it was imperative to promote this new way of thinking because the Ford system's emphasis on mass production resulted in waste along every step of the production process:

1. Waste arising from overproducing
2. Waste arising from time on hand (waiting)
3. Waste arising from transporting
4. Waste arising from processing itself
5. Waste arising from unnecessary stock on hand
6. Waste arising from unnecessary motion
7. Waste arising from producing defective goods

Together, these seven wastes result in tremendous losses and increase costs dramatically. Therefore, it was deemed necessary to completely eliminate waste in every way possible.

From that point on, the Toyota production system developed as the reversal of the preconceptions of the Ford system.

▸ Thinking of the production flow as a flow upstream

The flow of production is the moving of things — commonly forward. Therefore, to reverse this, we considered moving and transporting things backwards.

The existing way of thinking was to have the preceding process make things and provide them in succession to the subsequent process. What if we were to look at that flow of production backwards? Suppose:

The subsequent process withdraws from the preceding process exactly what it needs when it needs it.

In that case, what should the preceding process do?

The preceding process produces exactly the same quantity as is withdrawn.

It follows that the preceding process will go to its preceding process to withdraw exactly what it needs when it needs it, and so forth.

In this way, as we climb further and further up the production flow, ultimately the flow is reversed — not cut off. We might ask, what is the intrinsic significance of overturning conventional wisdom and reversing the production flow? It can be found in the marketplace.

All points of departure are from the marketplace. We have stated that the subsequent process goes to the preceding process to withdraw exactly what it needs when needed. In this scenario we must ask, what is the departure point for the last process? It is the point of contact with the many and diverse customers, the very pulse of the marketplace.

For passenger cars, the pulse is at the dealer's showroom, where either prospective new automobile buyers or existing owners desiring a trade-in come to decide on models. More precisely, it can be said that the exact contact is when the salesperson, with catalog in hand and equipped with the latest information, probes the customer for his or her exact needs.

Information from the concluded sales contracts immediately enters the dealer's computer system and is collected in the company's main host computer. From there it is analyzed, divided, and sent to the various production facilities. It is received by the final assembly process of those plants where finished cars are turned out. From there the information begins its climb up the hill of the production process.

We can divide the information into two main groups. One is within the production plant where it climbs the hill from subsequent processes to preceding processes. The other information group is dispersed to the various suppliers involved outside the plant where it climbs the production hill in the same way.

The *information flow* begins in the marketplace. Reversing the planned mass production flow prevalent since Henry Ford's day, in a sense, restores to information its natural flow.

▸ *Kanban* is information

Kanban is a control tool for the purpose of implementing JIT production, one of the two pillars of the Toyota production system. The most common form of kanban is a small slip of paper inserted in a rectangular vinyl pouch. While there is no need to restrict the form it takes, a kanban should indicate *what, when, and how much to withdraw* and *what, when, and how much to make*. The subsequent process withdraws from the preceding process exactly what it needs when it needs it. The preceding process supplies exactly that which has been withdrawn. This is the JIT production system. In this case, that which connects the two processes with withdrawal or transport information is called the *withdrawal kanban* or *transport kanban*. This is an important information function of kanban.

Another function is fulfilled by the *in-process kanban*, indicating to the preceding process mentioned above to produce exactly that amount which has just been withdrawn. These two functions are two sides of the same idea. *External kanban*, between processes and between plants, and *internal kanban*,

	Function	Rule
1	Provides withdrawal or transport information.	The subsequent process goes to the preceding process and withdraws only the amount of goods indicated by the kanban.
2	Provides production information.	The preceding process produces goods in the exact number and order withdrawn as indicated by the kanban.
3	Prevents overproduction or excess transport.	Do not produce or transport goods without a kanban.
4	Acts as a work order.	Always affix a kanban to goods.
5	Identifies process where defects are produced.	Do not allow defective goods to proceed down the line. This demands 100% perfection at every process.
6	Acts as a tool for inventory control and revealing problems.	Strive to reduce the number of kanban.

Table 1. Functions and Rules for the Use of Kanban

within processes and within plants, move around at a dizzying pace in the integrated system of Toyota and its suppliers.

There are circumstances in which other kinds of kanban can be created and utilized. It must be remembered, however, that they are meaningless unless tied to the primary goal of reducing costs and maximizing profits through the total elimination of waste. For this reason, it is essential that there be total commitment to kanban used as information.

▼

Dialogue A: An age where the information flow leads the production flow

Mito: In terms of an information flow, it is apparent that the flow does not start until the order is received at the market and the market needs are understood. Yet for a long time the production flow came thundering down on the marketplace like a waterfall. It was too one-sided.

When did the necessity to harmonize the production flow with the information flow become apparent?

Ohno: It was clearly during the first oil crisis in the fall of 1973. Until then, although there had been occasional plateaus since 1950, Japan's economic growth rate had been continuous. Production could never keep up with demand and companies found themselves in competition to produce the largest quantity in a given time period. The production plant became the battleground of "big guns and warships." Since it was a time when we could sell everything we could make, the deficiencies of "big guns and warships" management was not yet apparent. Instead, market shares increased and we became quite self-satisfied, basking in the praise showered on our companies. That was the pitfall of the times.

In any event, growth stopped and perhaps even declined the following year. It felt strange that Japan could actually experience negative economic growth. Our shock was great — as was the decline in business earnings.

It may seem obvious, but if we visualize the flow of economic development as waves, we find peaks as well as ebbs. If we maintain this overview and a proper perspective, then it should not be possible to run blindly into the trap of "big guns and warships" management.

▸ Waking up to "big guns and warships"

Mito: The faults of "big guns and warships" became visible at the time of the first oil crisis. But the shock Toyota received was clearly less dramatic than that received by other companies. Toyota received much attention in the industrial world, where it was thought there must be some trick or gimmick.

At this time, were the Toyota production system's two pillars, *just-in-time* and *autonomation*, already being practiced companywide?

Ohno: Toyota's founding chairman Toyoda Kiichirō issued a postwar challenge to the Japanese auto industry to catch up with America within three years or lose all chance of survival. It can be said that resistance to just-in-time began at that very point.

However, just-in-time and autonomation steadily permeated the organization in the early 1960s and continued to do so throughout the period of rapid growth. They were implemented gradually, with commitment to the principles serving as the background for establishing such manufacturing practices as (1) making one worker responsible for several processes, (2) dramatically reducing setup times for presses, and (3) rethinking the transport and withdrawal of goods. The function of kanban as information was steadily adopted between the production processes.

The use of *andon* (literally meaning "lanterns") to stop the assembly line in unusual circumstances was also established in 1961. This represents *visual control*, one of the unique practices of the Toyota production system. If it is necessary to stop the line to fix something, the worker just turns on the red light — and we tell workers that they should not hesitate to do so. Correcting defects is necessary to reach our goal of totally eliminating waste.

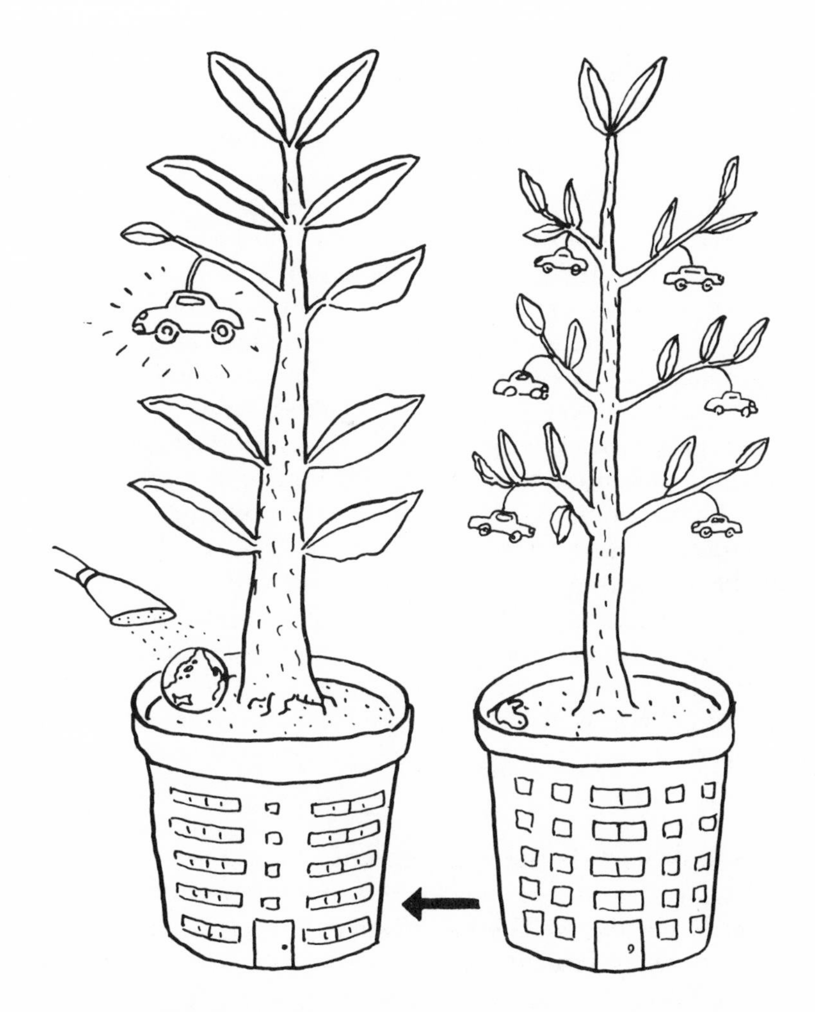

Figure 1. The pursuit of quantity cultivates waste while the pursuit of quality yields value.

Mito: To achieve this stated goal, it would seem necessary for more than just Toyota's people to rethink their old production methods. To make the system work, wouldn't you need to get not only Toyota affiliates but also supplier companies involved in the production revolution?

Ohno: During the 1973 oil crisis, everyone opened their eyes. In fact, even Toyota tended to follow the trend toward "mass production, mass sales," run for the "big guns and warships," and use high-volume machines to increase output. Remember that during the late 1960s and early 1970s it had been possible to sell anything made. However, since the Toyota people had already begun to realize the importance of purging every kind of waste, Toyota did not crowd the factory by installing new equipment to the extent other companies did.

Before the first oil crisis, Toyota's suppliers were not enthusiastic about the Toyota production system. For years I had taken every opportunity to explain the thinking behind the new manufacturing technology and define exactly what the Toyota system was — but I never received a positive response.

At the time, everyone thought the best strategy was to install highly efficient equipment for mass production and turn out high volumes. Surpluses could be stored in warehouses because certainly there would come a time when we could find a market. With the first oil crisis, these companies had a rude awakening trying to dispose of that inventory.

When Toyota's profits revived and increased in 1975 and 1976, the supplier companies began coming around to ask about the Toyota production system. It's funny how people don't get serious about something until they are confronted by necessity.

▸ Toyota's theme is my theme

Mito: Reflecting on Toyota's postwar history, I can't overlook the acute management crisis of 1950 and the big labor disputes of that time.

There was an extreme depression. It was a chaotic time when many employees were dismissed. Yet suddenly salvation came in the form of the extraordinary economic demand brought on by the Korean War. Did Toyota learn from experiencing the sense of crisis and the extreme fluctuations in business conditions?

Ohno: We might say that this was the beginning of postwar Toyota. In the midst of labor disputes, large personnel cuts, and an unprecedented management crisis, we had to think about how to rebuild the company and restore a sense of order to the factory floor.

Fortunately, the Korean War laid tremendous demands on the production plants. It was indeed like the divine winds that saved Japan from the ancient Mongol invaders. However, the new demand brought new problems — and we sought desperately to deal with them. We had just reduced our labor force due to lack of work and didn't feel we could add staff again just because suddenly we received some orders. Therefore we sought to sustain a higher volume with a smaller work force by eliminating as much wasted effort as possible.

Under these conditions we developed the JIT system through continuous trial and error. From one production department it spread to the whole plant and then to other plants in the system. It spread outside Toyota to related companies and suppliers.

It was really the oil crisis of 1973 that impressed upon us the need to have the Toyota production system extend outside the company and take root in suppliers and related companies, thus making it a true Toyota system. It took nearly 30 years after the war to reach this point.

Mito: It took that much time after Toyoda Kiichirō conceived of the JIT system?

Ohno: About the same time Toyoda Kiichirō issued his postwar challenge, Toyota's chairman Toyoda Eiji expressed the JIT philosophy: "In broad industries, such as automobile manufacturing, it is best to have the various parts arrive alongside the assembly line just-in-time."

As I have said before, JIT is having the needed goods arrive in the needed amount at the needed time. It is an extremely rational approach to eliminating waste and constitutes the basic philosophy of the Toyota production system. I was deeply inspired to hear these words come directly from the founder of the system himself. I remember having a vision flicker through my mind of a plant completely rooted in just-in-time — the perfect production facility.

This was Toyota's theme — and my personal one as well. From its defeat in World War II through reconstruction and rapid growth, and until the 1973 oil crisis, Japan was greatly influenced by foreign countries — as a nation, as businesses, and as individuals. This was a mixed blessing.

Japan learned a great deal about automobile manufacturing from the advanced nations — particularly the United States. Not everything learned, however, was suitable for Japan. Japan pursued the "big guns and warships" policies of the "mass production, mass sales" philosophy. In an economic period of continuous rapid growth, the defects in these policies are not apparent and indeed seem powerful.

However, when overcome by the first oil crisis, Japanese companies were at a loss. The long-hidden defects of the American-style "mass production, mass sales" management system surfaced at last.

▸ The source of information is always the customer — not the production plant

Mito: Business is essentially the interaction between the buyer and the seller. In the past as well as today, a transaction is complete upon conclusion of contract negotiations and the transfer of goods. Prices and market changes are determined by the relative strengths and weaknesses of supply and demand. This too is one of the fundamental principles of market economics. In the postwar era, Japan's ability to sell everything it could make ended with the first oil crisis. What caused this?

Ohno: Fundamentally, there was a change in attitude. The customer no longer came first — somehow the seller did. And this attitude became acceptable.

The essence of business is the seller's response to customer orders for certain products. This is market economics. However, it became common to think of information flowing because anything we made was being sold. This was the reverse order. Business was business and sellers paid little attention to customer preferences and psychology, regardless of their influence.

Mito: It seems, then, that the fault for the breakdown in relations between buyers and sellers lies with the latter. They simply couldn't grasp the purchasing motivations and values of their many and diverse customers.

Ohno: It is meaningless for salespeople to pass the buck by blaming poor business returns on a change in customer preferences.

A company's most important mission is to figure out how to sense inherently market changes — whether pleasurable or painful — and be organized for action. Only by doing this can it respond successfully to the marketplace. For this to happen, the seller company must undergo an attitude change.

We can classify sellers into three groups: (1) *producers* who make the products, (2) *retailers* who sell them directly to the customers, and (3) *wholesalers* who are in-between. During the era of rapid growth, the producers became too powerful.

Retailers, on the other hand, have delicate sensors that pick up bits of information in their direct contacts with customers. It would have been best had retailers, either directly or through wholesalers, rapidly passed on this information to producers. This did not happen, however, because of the balance of power between the two. It was a time when anything made could be sold and producers simply passed on to retailers whatever they felt like making. By supplying inexpensive products by using "big guns and warships" in the factory, they were able to keep both retailers and customers happy.

During this time, waste was hidden deeply within the companies. The most dangerous development, however, was producer attitude and the loss of the necessary sense of humility towards wholesalers, retailers, and customers. Producers exercised power by ignoring the flow of information (customer orders) and unilaterally passing on products to the market.

Mito: Relationships between producers, wholesalers, and retailers differ between industries. Even within the same industry we see some producers using wholesalers and some going directly to retailers. The striking development of the late 1960s and early 1970s was the arrival of mass sales outlets called "superstores" and the rise of a large service sector in many industries.

In this way, powerful retailers arose — some so powerful that they took the role of price setting away from the producers. But in the automobile industry, the sales networks were already firmly in place.

The large automobile assemblers, such as Toyota and Nissan, sit at the top of the pyramid. Many kinds of parts are delivered to their doors and fully assembled cars pass down to the sales networks with little effort. This makes these producers vulnerable to a critical buildup of useless inventory in bad times, not to mention crises such as the 1973 oil shock.

In an era when we could sell anything, it was most important to meet the market needs. Producers only had to produce to meet those needs. Toyota, too, endeavored as much as possible to fulfill every order. Of course, as you said earlier, it's not easy to instill JIT thinking during such times. Getting the JIT message across to all the Toyota departments must have been difficult.

Nevertheless, even incomplete JIT implementation at Toyota produced results. Thereafter, suppliers and related companies became serious about JIT. By the time of the second oil crisis, manufacturers were eager for information from the market and were able to respond quickly. The flow of information finally was being received properly.

▸ Responding individually to individual orders

Ohno: We came to believe it best to respond to information coming from the marketplace and to produce exactly what was needed when it was needed. However, it was impossible to change everyone's thinking immediately. People don't appreciate prosperity until they encounter adversity — and companies are the same. It wasn't until a recession was brought on by the oil crisis that companies came to their senses and reflected on the era of rapid growth. They then became serious about eliminating waste through just-in-time.

It must be noted that, in fact, rapid growth returned to the auto industry by the late 1970s. Japan's domestic market had indeed matured and growth flattened, but the export market — particularly to America — boomed. Statistics clearly show the situation. In 1975, Japan produced 4.57 million automobiles, of which 40 percent or 1.83 million were for export. By 1980, of the 7.03 million autos produced, 56 percent or 3.94 million were exported. Of the exports, 40 percent went to the United States.

Thus, enjoying growth through another export boom, the Japanese auto manufacturers tended to forget the pain of the earlier recession. Exports continued to climb until trade friction arose with Europe and the United States. As you know, from 1981 until the present there have been voluntary restraints on exports to the United States.

What I wish to clarify most here is that the market situation changed completely after the 1973 oil crisis. Since 1981, with the initiation of voluntary export restraints, domestic automobile production has reached a ceiling. Manufacturers are rushing to invest capital directly and erect plants in the United States. Meanwhile, the domestic market matures and changes.

Customer preferences are becoming more diverse, more personalized, and more rigid. Simply supplying the market with the same model produced in the same way can only result in a pile of useless inventory. In fact, customers differ totally from one another and base their purchases on personality. Strictly speaking, information delivered to the factory from the dealers will always be different, making it impossible to produce a single model to satisfy every order.

It becomes imperative, therefore, to think of a way to produce individually unique products in the factory. We can see that "planned mass production," namely, the Ford system, is not suited to this task since its premise is rapidly producing large quantities of the same item. Because customer orders are unique, the production line must produce unique items one by one. This way of thinking is natural if we put ourselves in the customer's place.

However, somewhere along the line this way of thinking was reversed. Thinking that pooling orders reduces costs is

Figure 2. Tastes differ from customer to customer. "This is my favorite flavor!"

ultimately a self-righteous attitude taken by the production plant. It produces tremendous waste. It is ridiculous to suggest that it reduces costs. It is safe to say that planned mass production is the instigator of the seven kinds of waste already mentioned — overproducing, time on hand, transporting, processing itself, unnecessary stock on hand, unnecessary motion, and producing defective goods.

We can expect customer orders to be unique. Furthermore, since the time, place, and circumstances of each order differ, it is impossible to foresee only one type of customer. To do so creates waste time after time. Since planned production is the ivory tower plan of someone who doesn't know the customer, it is not scientific at all.

These problems result from neglecting the fundamental truth that the source of information is the customer — not the production plant.

▸ Supermarkets exemplify just-in-time

Mito: Ford's planned mass-production system was a social system that symbolized America's "mass production, mass sales" society — a system that increasingly resulted in waste. American rationalism with its guiding principle of the consumer as king presupposed that prosperity followed merely from rapidly producing goods at low cost. In the end, however, it led to waste and a loss to society. Having achieved prosperity early on, American automobile manufacturers didn't try to accommodate the diversifying consumer tastes with a more flexible production style.

The Toyota production system was conceived to correct the defects of the Ford system. While not going as far as producing great diversity in small quantities, it did strive tenaciously to eliminate waste by producing a small number of models in small quantities.

What is extremely interesting, however, is that while you saw that introducing the Ford system to Japan would be a big mistake, you also were able to learn from another institution deeply rooted in American society — the supermarket. How did this happen?

Ohno: I don't think the Ford system is flawed fundamentally. Henry Ford developed his planned mass-production system after much trial and error at the beginning of the twentieth century. The Model T became the symbol of the mass-produced car. It was the birth of the automobile manufacturing industry and the beginning of global, large-scale manufacturing.

I will return to that point later, but the fact that the Ford system gave rise to the American "mass production, mass sales" society and the accompanying production of waste is not because Henry Ford made mistakes nor because the Ford system itself is wrong.

It is because Henry Ford's successors failed to fine-tune the system to enable it to adapt properly to changing times. I think if Henry Ford were alive today he would conceive of and implement a system very much like the Toyota production system.

After the war, information from America flooded Japan. In the midst of this flood, the image of the supermarket, closely intertwined with the life of the American consumer, left a deep impression on me. While I had only seen it in photographs, while turning over the image in my mind it struck me that the supermarket was exactly like the JIT system we were developing in Japan. In the abstract, the supermarket and just-in-time are exactly the same.

The supermarket is where customers go to buy exactly what they need when they need it. In this self-service system, they take a basket in hand at the entrance and go around picking out enough for today, tomorrow, perhaps a week. Sometimes they may, in fact, buy more than they need, but in principle it is a place to purchase only what is necessary. This was the type of supermarket on which we modeled our automobile plants.

The idea we got from supermarkets, stated directly, is as follows: *Assume the supermarket is the preceding process in the production line. The subsequent process (the customer) goes to the supermarket to get exactly what it needs (in the case of the automobile assembly plant, auto parts) when it needs it. What should the preceding process then do? It must replenish that which has been withdrawn by the subsequent process.*

By climbing back up the hill of the production process in this way, couldn't we create a smooth flow? From that starting point we went through a series of trials and errors, keeping in mind the image of the supermarket we had never seen.

Mito: I can see now the ideas you got from the supermarket and what your starting point was.

Breaking down the Toyota system, we start first with Toyota-style production. This is what creates the flow on the floor of the production plant. Traditionally, lathes were arranged with lathes, milling machines with milling machines, all designed to produce as much as possible of a single item.

In Toyota-style production, however, a flow is created by arranging lathes, milling machines, and drill presses one by one in the order of the processes and in the order that value is added. In this way you can shift from operations where one worker is responsible for one machine to operations where one worker is responsible for several machines. The result is a tremendous increase in productivity.

Another essential element of the Toyota system is the use of kanban to transmit information. Introducing the kanban system is a way of implementing JIT production — but how can we synthesize these two ideas?

▸ The supermarket is a strong social system

Ohno: It's not so complicated. The main point is that if the production flow is smooth then products low in cost and high in quality will emerge naturally. To say that the flow of production is smooth is to say, ultimately, that people have mastered the use of the machines. No matter how efficient the "big guns and warships" machines we introduce may be, it is a futile exercise if they are not mastered by the workers. If the worker doesn't notice when something has gone temporarily awry with the machine, a large number of defective goods will pile up.

Every machine is out of order sometimes. We must stop the machine — and in the case of an automobile plant, stop the assembly line — and fix the problem. Efficient automated equipment must have automatic stopping devices attached to reduce waste. This is what is meant by the second pillar of the Toyota production system — autonomation. We must exert endless energy to reduce waste to zero. And it is a tough enemy...

For that reason, as you pointed out, in the plant we must first rearrange the equipment in the order that people work and in the order that value is added to create a flow. In creating a flow, it is not enough to look at just part of the process. By thinking of and imagining the entire arrangement, we can come up with new ideas. This model applies not only within the plant or organization but outside to the various social systems as well.

People are always coming together and then going off on their own. Yet, there is order amidst this chaos — the supermarket, for one thing.

Mito: "The part and the whole" is a very philosophical concept. I think it is indispensable in thinking about the interaction of the individual and the organization, the company and society, or Japan and the world.

Systematic thinking is very strong in American society. Whether it is the flow of goods or the flow of information, the goal is to do everything as rationally and effectively as possible. As such a social system, the supermarket has deep roots in American society.

Is it possible to think of the Ford "mass production, mass sales" system and the supermarket as parts of the same whole?

Ohno: Whether goods or information, to get such a flow going we first must consider the big picture and create a system. The supermarket can be called a representative American social system. Moreover, since it dispassionately examines and sorts out the preferences of many diverse customers, we can say it is the strongest and most advanced system. Its having taken root in such a tumultuous environment speaks volumes about its strength.

My first sight when I visited an American town in 1956 was a supermarket. Customers went around the store with baskets and selected goods as they pleased. When finished, they checked out, paid at the cash register, and then left. Seeing this shopping flow with my own eyes, I felt as though my wishes had been granted.

▸ Using kanban in the supermarket...

Mito: Kanban is the method for implementing the Toyota production system. The first step in implementing Toyota-style production is to create a flow; next is to establish JIT production. To this end, kanban are used.

There are many kinds of kanban, but the most popular is a small slip of paper inserted in a vinyl pouch. Clearly recorded on the kanban is information indicating what, when, and how much to transport, and, similarly, what, when, and how much to produce.

Figure 3. The supermarket: we get exactly what we want when we want it.

In your book *Toyota Production System: Beyond Large-Scale Production* (Cambridge, Massachusetts: Productivity Press, 1988), you warn us that a little knowledge is a dangerous thing and that misusing kanban as a tool can yield disastrous results. To be sure, kanban is used to implement JIT, helping production occur exactly when needed. But the results will be terrible if a company takes advantage of a strong position to misuse kanban and demand immediate delivery of this, that, and the other thing. This is known as "bullying" by the large companies.

You emphasized that kanban be used to bring to light the various forms of waste and thereby facilitate their elimination — for example, suppressing waste arising from overproduction by using kanban. You further advocated using the power of kanban to reduce inventories, eradicate defects, reduce the number of processes, and prevent the recurrence of breakdown.

Also worthy of attention is your explanation of how kanban become the "autonomic nervous system" of the production plant, not only making clear the role of controllers and foremen but indicating to the workers themselves when operations should begin and when overtime is necessary. You explain the meaning of kanban as information.

How can we bring kanban into the metaphor of the supermarket?

▸ Withdrawal kanban and production kanban move quickly

Ohno: The latter process (the customer) purchases many goods and leaves. As a matter of course, a record is left at the cash register of the type, number, and value of the items purchased. The card on which they are recorded is the kanban sent to the preceding process (the purchasing department). In this way, items are replaced quickly.

The basic premise of the Toyota production system is the subsequent process withdrawing from the preceding process exactly what it needs when it needs it. This happens when the customer shops at the supermarket. At that time, what should the preceding process (the supermarket) do? As stated earlier, *the preceding process produces exactly the same quantity as is withdrawn.*

That is to say, the preceding process goes to its preceding process (the purchasing department) to withdraw that which was purchased by the customer. It has the purchasing department supply only that which was sold. The card used to transfer information in this process is the kanban and corresponds to the Toyota system's withdrawal kanban.

The goods on the store shelves correspond to the stock on hand on the factory floor. Assume for a moment that the supermarket has a nearby production department or supply base. Linked to the withdrawal kanban is a production kanban that is passed on to the supply base, which supplies or produces only that which was withdrawn (sold in the store).

Mito: It is clear that giving free flow to your imagination helped you use the image of the supermarket. Imagination moves freely between seemingly unrelated things and images, unleashing and intensifying long hidden powers of concentration, helping to solve problems. The connection between the Toyota production system and the supermarket is just such a solution.

Ohno: Humans are different from other animals in that if they have a problem to solve or a target to reach, the larger or more difficult it is, the harder they try. The human imagination is a strange thing.

Take, for example, the final assembly line of an automobile manufacturer. If we stand by and watch the line, we can understand the flow clearly. Each day several thousand units are produced. The flow is fast.

However, if we move from the final assembly line to the press department, we see steel sheets of various thicknesses being stamped out. The flow between the subsequent and preceding processes isn't felt as strongly as in the case of the final assembly line. But by paying close attention, we can see there is definitely a flow. There had never been a flow in the press department until it was connected with the final assembly line. Once connected, its flow is the same as that of final assembly.

From the late 1940s to the early 1960s, production quantities were small. Since numbers were small, all production moved in large batches from process to process. It became more of a "push" operation than a flow.

If we were to walk around the factory at that time we would see each process producing a separate flow as though it were a small independent enterprise. There would be no collaboration between adjacent processes. Nowhere would we see the spirit of a relay team in the baton-passing zone where runners skillfully pass the baton without slowing the pace. The relay team metaphor indicated how the flow of the total production plant ought to be.

The mind often attacks such problems. For example, at the Nagoya train station we see long lines at both the ticket-selling and the ticket-taking booths. We begin to wonder if the system would be more efficient if we added another booth or two, taking into consideration the fluctuations in number and types of passengers from day to day and hour to hour. If we add another booth, how many should we add? If we reduce the number, by how many? The human mind is always at work this way.

The United States consistently has been the object of Japanese fascination in the postwar era. Since the message "catch up with America," we were absorbed by anything made in America, be it supermarkets or whatever.

▼

Dialogue B: "In time" is not enough, it must be "just..."

Mito: Tell me more about why you were fascinated with the supermarket in particular. Its use as a metaphor for an automobile factory is very interesting.

Ohno: Automobile assemblers such as Toyota, when thinking about the flows of goods, production, and information within the production plant, must think simultaneously of those same flows entering and leaving the plant as well.

Put simply, the *internal flow* is when value is added to the parts brought in from outside as they are assembled into completed automobiles. In contrast, the *external flow* is the flow of parts and materials from various suppliers to Toyota and the shipping of completed automobiles to the retail market.

It was while thinking of the production plant in the middle of these "external-internal-external" flows that I heard about supermarkets. From a bird's-eye view in the marketplace, I saw the supermarket as flows of goods, production, and information.

Mito: From there, you went on to experiment with a supermarket-type setup in the plant. Wasn't that before you had seen the real thing in the United States?

Ohno: By 1953, Toyota had already set up various "stores" at each stage of the plant's manufacturing process. We experimented with the supermarket method of having no more than one unit at each process. At that time we began using small pieces of paper (kanban) to indicate the part number and information necessary for assembly. It was then that the phrase "kanban system" was born. The point of using the word "kanban" was to have a name unique to Toyota. We rejected foreign words as much as possible to keep foreigners from understanding and imitating the system.

After much trial and error, we were able to master the use of kanban as information. We knew we would be able to use kanban to unify, synchronize, and systematize not only movements within the plant but also movements in and out of the plant as well.

One glance at a scrap of paper can give us the production quantity, time, method, and order. The same goes for the transportation quantity, time, destination, method, and receptacle. We knew then that we had a superior information method.

Mito: The most valuable insight you obtained from the supermarket model was seeing how the production flow could be kept smooth. Information also can flow smoothly at the needed times, along with the needed goods. Human effort is never wasted.

Ohno: In most firms the work-in-process clerk types out various notices such as the "work-in-process plan," the "transporting plan," the "production plan," and the "delivery plan." When these are circulated through the plant, the most important point — *when* — is often interpreted casually. "As long as I finish in time, it's alright," or "It's OK to finish ahead of time," and so forth.

When this happens you need more people than otherwise would be necessary to manage the surplus inventory created. This is not "just-in-time." There is too much waste. The true meaning of "just-in-time" is in the "just." We cannot eradicate waste merely by following an "in-time" policy.

In the Toyota production system, waste arising from overproduction is completely suppressed through the widespread use of kanban as information. The necessity for a warehouse to store the surplus and a clerk to manage the warehouse and all the accompanying paperwork is eliminated.

▸ The inventory argument of Itoh Masatoshi, president of Itoh Yokado, a successful retail chain

Mito: Before you ever saw a supermarket, you gained many insights from it and, in fact, continued to use it as a model even later on.

As a system, Toyota's production methods came together during the period of rapid growth from the late 1950s to the early 1970s. By the first oil crisis in 1973 the system drew the attention not only of the automobile industry but of other industrial circles as well. The discussion you had then with Itoh Masatoshi, President of Itoh Yokado, was extremely interesting.

Ohno: In early 1975, when Mr. Itoh came to Toyota headquarters to ask how we reduced inventories, he said:

"It is especially difficult to eliminate inventories in the distribution industry — or even maintain an appropriate inventory level. If we strive to reduce inventories to zero, we may lose the customer to a competitor in the process."

Mito: That's just like Mr. Itoh. Of all the distribution enterprises, only Itoh Yokado showed restraint during the rapid growth era and didn't run wildly after increased volume and revenue. From beginning to end, it emphasized guaranteed profits resulting from quality management and the total elimination of waste. It's just like him to seek you out after the first oil shock when many other executives were running around in confusion.

Ohno: Even though I should have been learning from him, he prepared several questions and took notes diligently in a notebook. I was humbled by his attitude. With his sharp mind, he took difficult business problems and tried to solve them. His imagination gave birth to new concepts and systems.

Mito: What did you discuss? Following the oil shock, wasn't it a critical period for both Itoh Yokado and Toyota Motors?

▸ Zero inventories is nonsense!

Ohno: To be sure, if we completely eliminate inventories, we will have shortages of goods and other problems. In fact, reducing inventories to zero is nonsense.

The goal of the Toyota production system is to level the flows of production and goods. In every plant and retail outlet, we strive to have the needed goods arrive in the needed quantities at the needed time. In no way is the Toyota production system a zero-inventory system.

I told Mr. Itoh that it was important to strive to reduce necessary inventory to a near-zero level. Mr. Itoh said that, while it depended on the product, in most cases three months' inventory was necessary.

At that point I said, "How would it be if we carefully checked the contents of the warehouses? I imagine there is very little or no inventory of the things that can be sold today. On the other hand, I venture to say there is up to six months' inventory of things gathering dust that cannot be sold. The average is indeed three months."

Mr. Itoh's reply was, "It is exactly as you say."

The point is to check carefully the origin of goods that don't sell and assure that the source, be it the wholesaler or production plant, gets connected to the flow from the marketplace where customer contact occurs.

A mass retailer like Itoh Yokado will find this more difficult to implement than a manufacturer like Toyota. For this reason, another mass retailer, the supermarket, continuously talks to many wholesalers and manufacturers. It must get them to agree to provide only what is needed in the needed amount at the needed time.

Mr. Itoh inferred that necessity early on. Positioned at the nerve center of the marketplace, in direct contact with customer needs, retailers like Mr. Itoh are the most important source of information for wholesalers and manufacturers. They take the lead in an information society.

The Itoh Yokado Group, which includes large retail outlets, fast-food chains, and convenience stores, has consistently demonstrated high earnings. This may be due to the fact that it realizes it is not merely a retailer but an information source as well.

Mito: We can see from your discussion with Mr. Itoh that, after the first oil crisis, interest in the Toyota production system spread not only throughout secondary industries but through tertiary industries, such as mass retailers, as well.

Today convenience stores are penetrating the customers' neighborhoods and providing 24-hour availability of desired products. The point-of-sale (POS) systems used there are powerful weapons. They are information systems that provide only needed goods at needed times.

POS systems are used not only in convenience stores. Itoh Yokado has taken the lead in Japanese industry by installing them throughout the entire group in preparation for the advent of the Information Age.

It feels as though, having fulfilled the basic principles of the Toyota production system, we are entering an age where we surpass that system and grope for an even better way.

▾

Mito's Commentary

▸ Toyoda Kiichirō, seeking an original Japanese Japanese production system to surpass the Ford system, developed just-in-time

In November 1935, Toyota Motors announced its pilot automobile at a ceremony in Shibaura, Tokyo. Toyoda Kiichirō (1894–1952) drew attention when he repeated the following remarks from his father, Toyoda Sakichi. "My father said, 'I built looms for the good of the country. You build automobiles. Build automobiles for the good of the country!'"

On March 27, 1952, before the automobile industry grew in earnest, Toyoda Kiichirō passed away. It is clear from many surviving documents that he himself came up with the uniquely Japanese concept of just-in-time production. No one denies that scientific and rational "Toyota-ism" was established by him. The criteria he prescribed for the shape of the auto industry are as follows:

- To produce a car for the mass market.
- To perfect passenger car manufacturing.
- To produce a car at a price that will sell.
- To strengthen sales by invigorating manufacturers' planning.
- To manufacture basic materials.

Toyoda Kiichirō pointed out that an automobile industry depends upon many other basic industries. This dependence necessitates a strong, wide base in science and research. For that reason he hoped strongly for close cooperation between industry and academe.

More than anyone else, Toyoda Kiichirō sought fervently to learn the fundamentals of automobile manufacturing from America's General Motors and Ford. With the basics from the United States and comparative Japanese resources, he hoped to create a Japanese-style method of manufacturing automobiles. He did not try simply and narrow-mindedly to imitate the Ford system.

In 1933, he set out a policy to develop a domestically manufactured mass-market automobile. One part of that policy was as follows. "We will learn American-style mass production methods but will not imitate them blindly. In the spirit of research and creativity, we will conceive a production system in keeping with the resources of our country." There is no doubt that the just-in-time system resulted from Toyoda Kiichirō's mastery of, first, basic technology and, then, manufacturing technology.

We can fully imagine that this just-in-time arrangement concealed the point of departure for the Toyota production system, a concept to surpass the Ford system. Today moreover, new ideas are floating on the horizon even while the just-in-time system itself is being further developed. The JIT concept is spreading quickly through industries of various kinds and sizes and across national borders. The driving force is its understanding of the structural changes accompanying the advance toward an information society.

▸ Toyoda Eiji took the lead in developing the Toyota production system

"The Roots of Kanban," an article by Toyota chairman Toyoda Eiji (1913–), is fascinating in its concise description of how the kanban system was made to work at Toyota. Mr. Ohno reported to him during his entire 35 years with Toyota. We can see the historical significance in the following excerpts from that work:

> We decided to introduce assembly-line production at the Kariya plant at the same time we adopted the metric system. To implement this, Toyoda Kiichirõ produced a detailed pamphlet. He had the assembly line in his mind even before the plant was built.
>
> We took semi-finished products ready to be planed and temporarily stored them in the warehouse. Tickets came around indicating how much of each individual part to produce. After that came instructions to drill holes. This was the so-called lot production method. But Mr. Toyoda's idea was to convert all this to assembly-line production, thereby eliminating the piles of goods and the need for the warehouse. The quantities of work in progress decreased and more money stayed in the company. To state it in reverse, we sold what we bought before we paid for it — so we had no need for working capital.
>
> A summary of this production system would be: Every day produce exactly what is needed in the quantity needed. To implement this system every process must become part of an assembly line whether it likes it or not. The phrase "just-in-time" is a prod-

uct of Toyoda Kiichirō's Japanese-English. The original English is "just-on-time." The essential meaning is "Do it on schedule. Don't produce surplus!" There were no kanban at the time, but each morning the day's production came around on a ticket. If the amount was produced ahead of time, everyone could go home early. If not, overtime was necessary.

How should the assembly-line way of thinking be instilled in the company? First, the employees — particularly the controllers and foremen — must be educated thoroughly. Because of such a revolutionary change, the old way of thinking about production must be eliminated. The pamphlet Toyoda Kiichirō produced was 10 centimeters [4 inches] thick and described in great detail the workings of the assembly line. These are the roots of the Toyota production system.

Toyota has used the words "just-in-time" ever since. The system that Toyoda Kiichirō wanted to instill even to the extent of brainwashing employees was put on hold with the outbreak of World War II. To revive the dormant system after the war became the work of Mr. Ohno. His method was kanban.

When the Koromo plant was completed, I was made responsible for setting it up. My job was to station myself in the plant and implement an assembly-line process. We finished three plants — the first made engines, the second made parts to attach to the engines, and the third made other parts. There were three plant managers in each plant. Of those three, one was to be an inspection manager. The idea was that when inspection turned up a defect the process producing that defect should be corrected immediately. The inspection manager should not only separate defects from the good products but also search out machines, equipment, and tools that would help prevent future defects.

After the war, we studied and enthusiastically introduced quality control (QC). The "quality" in quality control was to be produced "in the process," so it was essentially the same as Toyoda Kiichirō's initial thought — he wasn't a genius. The key is that he pushed implementation as far as possible.[1]

In fact, the phrase "just-in-time" is not Japanese-English — it is a phrase used by Americans as well. But to express Mr. Ohno's meaning precisely, perhaps the phrase "exactly-in-time" should be used.

▸ Charles E. Sorensen, who worked closely with Henry Ford, faithfully recorded the experiments leading to the creation of the Ford system

The way Mr. Ohno used the image of the U. S. supermarket in the process of developing the Toyota production system is explained in the initial dialogue section of this chapter. At any time or in any country the production plant is always a place for trial and error. New ideas are limited only by the degree of willingness to try them out immediately. At Toyota, we originally tried setting up the interior of the plant as a supermarket. Parts flowing through production would be like goods flowing through the store.

Henry Ford's system, also called planned mass production, was also the product of ambitious experimentation. Charles E. Sorensen, once a top Ford executive, has written in detail about its development. He was a head of the manufacturing department and assumed leadership of the company when Henry Ford passed away, forming a bridge between the reigns of Henry Ford I and Henry Ford II.

He was extraordinarily self-confident with his "we did it by ourselves" mentality. His writings overflow with suggestions that really give an understanding of the departure point of the Ford system.

> As may be imagined, the job of putting the car together was a simpler one than handling the materials that had to be brought to it. Charlie Lewis, the youngest and most aggressive of our assembly foremen, and I tackled this problem. We gradually worked it out by bringing up only what we termed the fast-moving materials. The main bulky parts, like engines and axles, needed a lot of room. To give them that space, we left the smaller, more compact, light-handling material in a storage building on the northeast corner of the grounds. Then we arranged with the stock department to bring up at regular hours such divisions of material as we had marked out and packaged.
>
> This simplification of handling cleaned things up materially. But at best, I did not like it. *It was then that the idea occurred to me that assembly would be easier, simpler, and faster if we moved the chassis along, beginning at one end of the plant with a frame and adding axles and the wheels; then moving it past the stockroom, instead of moving the*

> *stockroom to the chassis*. I had Lewis arrange the materials on the floor so that what was needed at the start of assembly would be at that end of the building and the other parts would be along the line as we moved the chassis along. We spent every Sunday during July planning this. Then one Sunday morning, after the stock was laid out in this fashion, Lewis and I and a couple of helpers put together the first car, I'm sure, that was ever built on a moving line.
>
> We did this simply by putting the frame on skids, hitching a towrope to the front end and pulling the frame along until axles and wheels were put on. Then we rolled the chassis along in notches to prove what could be done. While demonstrating this moving line, we worked on some of the sub-assemblies, such as completing a radiator with all its hose fittings so that we could place it very quickly on the chassis. We also did this with the dash and mounted the steering gear and the spark coil.[2]

To confirm hypotheses through experimentation is not confined to the academic world. In industry as well, ideas are tested through continuous trial and error. It is clear from Mr. Sorensen's experiences that the Ford system is the result of many experiments. It is interesting that the imaginative powers of Mr. Ohno, Henry Ford, and Charles Sorensen have in common the philosophy of managing from the workplace.

▸ The total elimination of waste, basis of the Toyota production system, owes itself to Toyoda Sakichi's "superrationalism"

The concept and implementation of autonomation, or "automation with a human touch" originated with the invention of the automatic loom by Toyoda Sakichi (1867–1930), one of Toyota's founders. His automatic loom was set up to stop automatically if a vertical thread broke or a horizontal thread for some reason did not appear. In other words, devices were installed that made a machine responsible for judging good and bad. It follows that there could be no production of defective goods.

Granted, many machines start automatically with the touch of a switch. With the increasing efficiency and speed of such machines, should something unusual occur, for example should some extraneous material find its way into the machine, in no time at all a huge mountain of defective goods will pile up. Furthermore, the machine may break, the tap snap, or other serious problems develop.

The meaning of autonomation is in machines with automatic stopping devices installed. For example, the stopping-in-fixed-positions policy, the full-work system, the foolproof system, and the *baka-yoke* system all have safety devices added to them. The machines are endowed with intelligence — or, as we say, have a human touch.

Giving automation a human touch also significantly changes the role of control. There is no reason to station a person at a machine that is operating smoothly. Only when there is a problem and the machine has stopped is a person needed at its location. Consequently, one person can manage several machines. The amount of labor is reduced and productivity increases by leaps and bounds.

How was Toyoda Sakichi able to harness the power of his imagination and formalize and systematize his thoughts? His way of looking at things and his attitude are described in the book *Conversations with Toyoda Sakichi* by Haraguchi Akira. In the following passage, he reflects on the spring of 1887 when he was 20 years old.

> The textile industry at that time was not as large as today's. Mostly, older women wove at home by hand. In my village, every family farmed and had a hand loom. That I came around to thinking about making a loom was probably a product of my environment. Sometimes I would spend all day watching the grandmother next door weaving. I came to understand the way the loom worked as it wound the woven cotton fabric into a thicker and thicker roll. The more I watched, the more interested I became.[3]

From the same book we see he was a man of great effort as well as of genius.

> He would not read catalogues or books. He would not borrow from newspapers or magazines. He never asked for information or borrowed from others to help in an invention. He never

> studied mathematics or physics. His thinking and inventing were accomplished completely by himself. No mathematics teacher or mechanical expert could find fault with his inventions. His logic fit all scientific principles.
>
> Because his inventions sprang directly from actual practice, they did not always follow scientific principles. In application, however, his inventions produced better results. He put his ideas into actions, not words.
>
> He didn't use consultants or assistants. He was independent and alone. He did not have a special research lab or any reference materials at his side. The living room in his home was his laboratory and office. He had no visitors and he wouldn't call on anyone. From morning till night, he would sit in the room, looking up at the ceiling and down at the surface of the mattress, pondering things quietly. In this way, he generated over one hundred patents.[4]

Toyoda Sakichi first visited the United States in 1910 when the automobile industry was rising to prominence. The popularity of automobiles was increasing and many industrialists were rushing into automobile production. Henry Ford had begun mass producing the Model T two years earlier.

Cars appeared on the market one after the other. Toyoda Sakichi must have been thrilled at the sight of it. He probably foresaw the day that cars would achieve mass popularity in Japan as well. By the time he returned home, he constantly was saying the automobile age was next.

▸ The two pillars of the Toyota system, just-in-time and autonomation, create a synergy between individual skill and teamwork

If we can master production of exactly what is needed when it is needed, then waste (*muda*), unevenness (*mura*), and unreasonableness (*muri*) can be eliminated from the workplace. Productivity will increase dramatically. Toyoda Kiichirō conceived of this system. With Mr. Ohno, he created the just-in-time system and saw the marketplace as the primary source of information.

The other pillar of the Toyota production system, autonomation, prevents defects by endowing machines with intelligence.

The inspiration for this came from another founder and great inventor — Toyoda Sakichi. The loom he designed stopped automatically if a thread broke because he built into it the power to discriminate. Toyota has taken this way of thinking and adapted it not only to its machines but to its operators as well — so if something goes wrong, no one should hesitate to stop the assembly line.

How should the relationship between the two pillars of the Toyota system be explained? Mr. Ohno uses the baseball metaphor to explain this in his earlier book, *Toyota Production System.*

> Using the analogy of a baseball team, autonomation corresponds to the skill and talent of individual players while just-in-time is the teamwork involved in reaching an agreed-upon objective.
>
> For example, a player in the outfield has nothing to do as long as the pitcher has no problems. But a problem — the opposing batter getting a hit, for instance — activates the outfielder who catches the ball and throws it to the baseman "just-in-time" to put the runner out.
>
> Managers and supervisors in a manufacturing plant are like the team manager and the batting, base, and field coaches. A strong baseball team has mastered the plays; it can meet any situation with coordinated action. In manufacturing, the production team that has mastered the just-in-time system is exactly like a baseball team that plays well together.
>
> Autonomation, on the other hand, performs a dual role. It eliminates overproduction, an important waste in manufacturing, and prevents the production of defective products. To accomplish this, standard work procedures, corresponding to each player's ability, must be adhered to at all times. When abnormalities arise — that is, when a player's ability cannot be brought out — special instruction must be given to bring the player back to normal. This is an important duty of the coach.
>
> In the autonomated system, visual control, or "management by sight," can help bring production weaknesses — in each player, that is — to the surface. This allows us then to take measures to strengthen the players involved.
>
> A championship team combines good teamwork with individual skill. Likewise, a production line where just-in-time and autonomation work together is stronger than other lines. Its power is in the synergy of these two factors.[5]

To develop teamwork, the competition between players must be eliminated and a spirit of mutual cooperation created. The Toyota system endeavors to instill a team atmosphere naturally by having workers develop skills in several areas.

Mr. Ohno's greatest reward was following in the footsteps of Toyoda Sakichi and Toyoda Kiichirō. The synergy between these two men forms the basis of just-in-time and autonomation.

▸ Rising from the demands of the time and changing market needs, Toyota's production system surpassed Ford's by staying flexible as the environment changed

The Toyota production system has been introduced in various firms and industries throughout Japan as well as in Southeast Asia, the United States, and Europe. Although its development is not yet complete, it clearly succeeds the Ford system. For this reason, practitioners everywhere strive daily to fine-tune its various elements.

In contrast, the Ford system was complacent — it believed itself king of the factory. Managers abdicated their opinions to the status quo without responding to the obvious changes in the marketplace. The 1973 oil crisis was the single event that transferred manufacturing leadership to the Toyota production system.

Let's compare the Toyota system to the Ford system (see Table 2 on the next page).

▸ Itoh Masatoshi has long contemplated how to provide customers with exactly what they want when they want it

The similarities between the founding president of Itoh Yokado, Itoh Masatoshi, and Mr. Ohno are great. They both listen carefully to what other people say and do ordinary things in a commonsensical way.

Toyota	Ford
Just-in-time and autonomation are the foundation of a system that provides exactly what is needed when it is needed.	A planned mass-production system in which the production process does not flow.
A *pull* system. The marketplace "pulls" necessary items from the factory.	A *push* system. The company does market research, makes a production plan, and "pushes" products onto the marketplace.
Adheres to production leveling in principle. Progressing from producing small lots of many models to producing unique items one at a time.	A stubborn adherence to production leveling. Identical to "mass production, mass sales" with its emphasis on producing similar items in large lots.
Pursues small-lot production on the factory floor. Emphasizes reducing machine setup times to 10 minutes and increasing their frequency.	Pursues large lots. Strives to reduce the number of setups in order to increase output per unit of time.
First, create a production flow. Next, use kanban as a method to produce just-in-time.	Mountains of work in process are created at each stage. Production does not flow but is pushed through.
One person is responsible for several machines or processes requiring multi-skilled rather than single-skilled workers.	One worker handles one process. Only a single skill is required and unions assign job descriptions.
Stopping the assembly line in order to prevent mass-producing defects is encouraged. Autonomated machines have automatic stopping devices.	Stopping the assembly line is discouraged even though mass-producing defects creates a mess.
The amount produced equals the amount sold.	The amount produced is based on ivory-tower calculations set forth in the production plan. It always leads to overproduction and defective goods.
The unique Toyota-style information system grasps the marketplace's *Now!* needs, suppressing overproduction. Kanban supply just enough production information moving backwards from final process to preceding processes.	Information floods the production plant because the production plan is sent to every process.

Table 2. Toyota Production System versus the Ford System

Mr. Ohno has mentioned how Mr. Itoh visited him soon after the first oil crisis. They discussed the latter's concept of "appropriate inventory" that greatly influenced the former's thinking.

Mr. Itoh is a modest man and has written only one book, titled *Business Considerations*. In it he says, "If there is something about the company I don't know, I ask a subordinate. If there is something outside the company I don't know, I ask an expert. If I don't know what is selling in the market, I go out and look for myself."

He posts the following "Four Considerations in Making Transactions" in every office of the company. They may seem ordinary at first glance, but fulfilling them is more difficult than we might imagine.

1. Itoh Yokado survives only because it has customers.
2. We will always keep our promises in transactions.
3. We will not be guests to our partners in transactions.
4. We will not sell returned goods.

The Itoh Yokado Group is diversified. In addition to Itoh Yokado itself, it consists of the Denny's restaurant chain, the 7-Eleven convenience stores, and the new Robinson department stores. Common to all of these enterprises is an "old yet new" atmosphere that arises from the determination to master the fundamentals of the business and go to any lengths to meet market needs.

Postwar Japanese businesses absorbed many good things — and some not so good — from America. This goes for the distribution industry as well, the most successful case being Itoh Yokado. We can learn much from studying the 7-Eleven convenience stores, so well positioned to compete in the coming Information Age.

The number two man in the Itoh Yokado Group is Suzuki Toshifumi. His "combination play" was to take everything the American 7-Eleven group had to offer in terms of systems and manuals and endow it with his own originality. That is clear from examining any 7-Eleven store in Japan.

In his writings, Itoh Masatoshi speaks of the adaptation of Denny's to the Japanese market. He says they went through

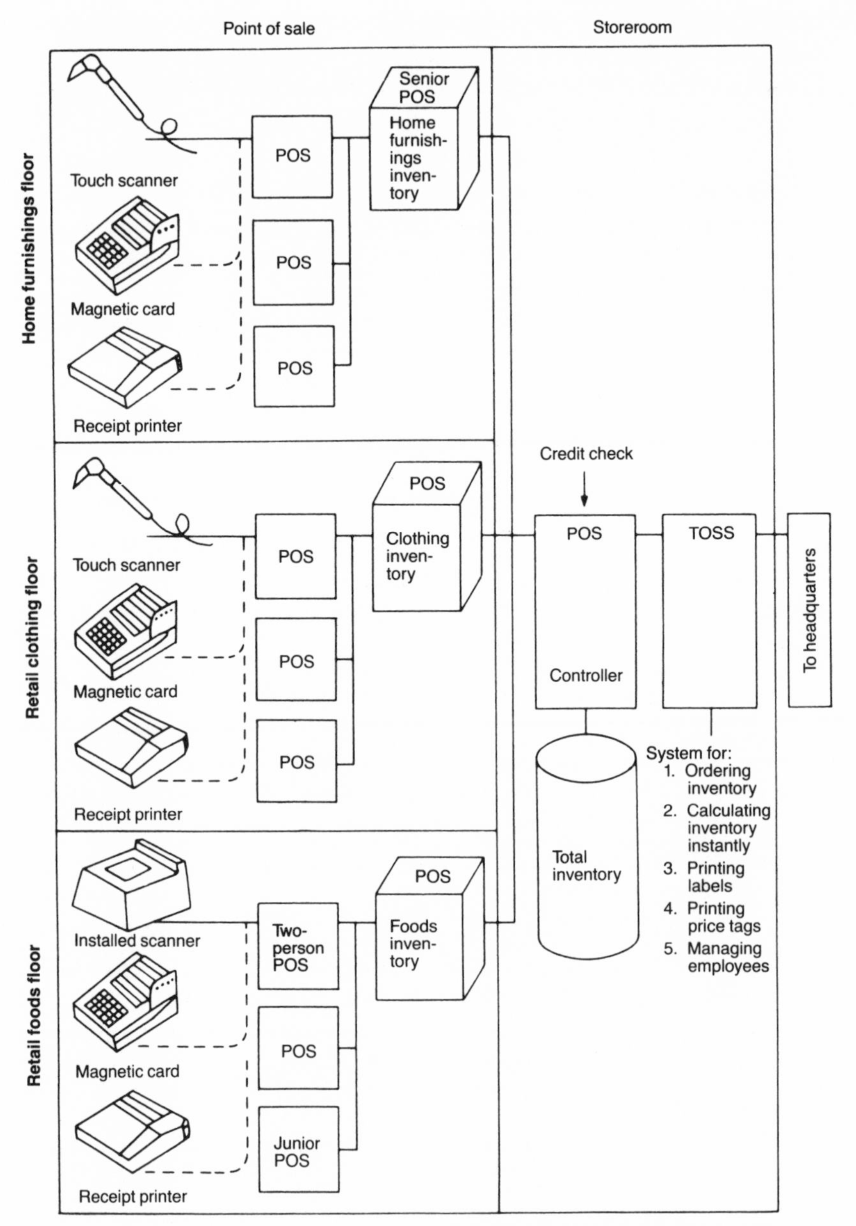

From: The Itoh Yokado Group Quarterly, Winter 1985.

Figure 4. Overview of the Itoh Yokado Point-of-Sale (POS) System

much trial and error to combine Japanese taste with American service. He also describes how long it took to establish the concept of the 24-hour convenience store in Japan, which of course everyone now takes for granted.

> I brag that our system and product arrangement is second to none, not even America's. It may sound as though we jumped to the top level in the world promptly after importing the know-how, but that is not the case at all. That will take another five or ten years. People change their habits slowly. Therefore, even if we introduce something new, ultimately it will take several years before customers grow accustomed to it.
>
> For example, 7-Eleven first began offering breakfast ten years ago. It didn't sell as well as we expected. For the most part, people didn't notice that we were open at 7 a.m. and selling breakfast at a place that wasn't a cafeteria. Also, because stores were few in number, we couldn't serve a large market. Today the idea is completely accepted. It so happens that the Japanese boxed-lunch services are also doing their best business now. I secretly think this is due to 7-Eleven's influence.
>
> We are endeavoring to create an information flow between other members of the Group. The 'Corporate Conference' was inaugurated in fiscal 1983 to enable the 28 member companies to exchange information on finance, store openings, products, new projects, and other general management information. In this way, the 7-Eleven management system is being introduced in stores throughout the Group.[6]

Itoh Masatoshi has stamped out the possibility of becoming overly reliant on bureaucratic systems. His entrepreneurial spirit seeks to absorb only the advantages of such systems. In November 1985, Itoh Yokado installed point-of-sale (POS) systems in every department of all 124 stores — and thus entered the Age of Management Systems.

2

Management's Power to Grasp and Act on the Now! *Needs of the Marketplace*

Theme: Not the past or future but the *Now!*

The Ford system was one of the moving forces behind the modernization of U. S. industry and the arrival of the American Century. Mass production was a powerful means to reduce costs and popularize the automobile, a product of modern civilization with its seemingly unlimited possibilities.

The system that Henry Ford developed has been called technically "assembly based on a flow system," but perhaps it is most appropriately described as a "planned mass-production system." That word "planned" has such a profound meaning that indeed we may call it a villain. Let me explain. In the case of the Ford system, "planned" means to strive to maximize the quantity produced within a given time period. This reduces costs and thereby lowers the price to the consumer, which in turn popularizes the automobile making it easier to sell. This is the plan in theory.

In terms of popularizing the automobile, however, Alfred P. Sloan of General Motors outrivaled Henry Ford's Model T. He saw the marketplace's coming diversification and successfully upgraded the popular car through a strategy of product differentiation. This created a new era in competition. But in manufacturing terms, he was unable to surpass Ford's planned mass-production system.

Mass production accelerates the shift from human labor to production by machines. Its goal is to reduce costs and make production as simple as possible.

Systems design in the twentieth century — such as the one established and popularized by Henry Ford — was based on an overall view of assembly of finished goods in a continuous production flow, rather than a partial view of individual parts, machines, or factories. This was just one of the complete systems of "mass production, mass sales" that brought modern manufacturing into a new age.

After its defeat in World War II, Japan began the process of rebuilding its economy and reentering international society. In the process, it developed manufacturing and management systems suited to Japanese markets. Of course, there were many visible signs of a mini-American-style consumer market rising from its postwar ruins. This was in part responsible for the country's rapid economic growth up until the 1973 oil crisis.

Masses of consumers stormed the market with ever-increasing demands for material satisfaction. It goes without saying that companies supplying those needs rushed to imitate the planned mass production of the Ford system. But regardless of how booming market demands may have been, it was not necessarily wise to copy exactly American-style mass production.

Even putting aside the issue of the different size and character of the Japanese market, we would have expected Japanese companies at least to strive to improve that system before adopting it. They should have modified it to suit their own market and industry conditions.

However, these companies did not do this during their time of expansion. They rushed headlong into the "big guns and warships" mentality; that is, to have the most mass-production equipment. In any case, with the possibility of selling anything they could make, Japanese companies "pushed" production onto the marketplace.

There are limits to material growth, however. At some point, it must stop or even reverse, which is precisely what happened after the first oil crisis. The starting point for the Toyota production system was recognizing that the Ford system was not necessarily the best for managing the highs and lows of material growth.

Here are the basic precepts underlying the Toyota production system:

1. Material growth is limited. It will rise, eventually decline, and approach zero.

2. Economic activity produces waves of all sizes. Waste necessarily will be created in the production activities of companies producing to meet these waves.

3. Putting aside for now the original intent of its creator, the Ford system's planned mass production in fact does produce production waste during prosperity — although it remains hidden. During recession, overproduction becomes apparent.

4. American management and its planned mass production is too often ivory-tower theory and backward looking.

5. No matter how great the market demand, each customer is different and has unique preferences. American planned mass production creates complacent suppliers who are unable to respond to needs of the marketplace and individual customers.

6. A *push* system cannot meet market needs. A *pull* system is required so customers pull from the factory exactly what they need when they need it. A *planned* system is no more than an ivory-tower theory ignoring market trends and relying too much on market research and other past information.

The theme of the Toyota production system is not the past, not the future, but the current *Now!* needs of the marketplace and customer. Although extremely difficult to grasp, the *Now!* needs must drive the organization. The process of developing the Toyota production system is the history of pursuing that goal.

The approaching Information Age brings with it the management possibility of grasping the *Now!* information coming from the marketplace.

▸ The convenience store grasps the *Now!*

I think the convenience store is an inevitable product of the Information Age. By answering the needs of the times, it has taken root as a social and a business system. The convenience store conceals a great deal of human imagination at work.

Being 1,000 square feet at most, it appears at first to be nothing more than a mini-supermarket. But, as implied, it is above all "convenient" for the customer. We don't make it a point to go every evening, but if we feel like getting a copy of a recent magazine we can find one easily at the convenience store. Next to the magazines is hot coffee, which we drink if we feel like it. We easily can start up a conversation with the shopkeeper and discuss what is selling well and so forth.

We may be surprised to discover that this little shop contains anywhere from 3,000 to 3,500 items. This number would include many relatively new products, of which 6,000 to 7,000 make their appearance during the course of a year. The substitution of these "players" is so rapid that it is said that over a two-year period the entire stock is new.

A position on the starting lineup of a professional baseball team may be hard to hold, but competition is much more severe for a position on the convenience store shelf. The product life cycle is very short. While not clear whether or not consumers' tastes change at such a dizzying pace, it is clear that the competition among retailers to meet those tastes is severe. We can imagine that the pressure must be intense.

With this intense competition the mind goes to work with different management strategies and puts out all sorts of new products. The results are many kinds of products: some good, some grotesque, some fraudulent. But in the end, those not up to snuff are weeded out by the consumers.

In market competition, sellers strive to grasp that quality of "salability" necessary for success in the marketplace. Negotiation between the customer and the seller (the chooser and the chosen) is a synergistic process that gives birth to salability and often produces a popular product.

What I would like to put forth as a hypothesis here is that what was pursued as salability until now is nothing more than past information and is, in fact, useless. Using that information leads to the production of mountains of unsalable goods. We will come back to the issue of how to grasp and use salability. But for now let us realize that it is not simple to implement a management system in which products are continually changed. A high degree of management skill and management technology is necessary.

Point-of-sale (POS) information management systems are being introduced enthusiastically in the distribution and financial industries. In convenience stores also terminals are being installed to enable the headquarters to gain precise minute-by-minute information on sales trends. Looking at this situation, we think that in some way the *Now!* of the market is being grasped. It now would seem possible to use this information in developing new products. Yet, this method failed to hold true long ago.

In fact, at the end of this exciting salability and information waits a pile of unsalable inventory. This was discovered by the auto industry when it encountered the negative growth brought on by the 1973 oil crisis. The auto companies presumed that they could sell whatever they made and that demand was unlimited. They competed to see who could install the most efficient equipment and produce the greatest quantity of goods in any given time period. The receiver of this unlimited output was the dealer who became the source of information on salability.

Yet salability became "unsalability" in the face of the first oil crisis, and a new way to find true salability could not be found. Salability in fact was not *Now!* information — it merely traced past trends.

Convenience stores have thought up a clever way to avoid this danger and grapple successfully with the *Now!*. What we might call the originality of the convenience stores is that they do not get carried away with information about salability. Rather, they focus on that which does not sell, thereby grasping thoroughly the nature of unsalability. They then mercilessly remove those products from the shelves.

By rapidly removing such products, they make space available for products developed with information on salability. In this way, salability is not completely useless. The *Now!* is realized by creating empty shelves based on understanding unsalability, a cycle that allows the shopkeeper to create continuously an energetic *Now!* atmosphere in the store.

It is dangerous to chase salability too closely because it is based on past information. A forecast of the future is also based on past information. The most important information to understand is the present. But is it really possible to grasp the *Now!*? If we think we have grasped it, is it alright to put that understanding in the shape of a new product and launch it in the marketplace? Undeniably, the convenience store is the model for dealing with and living in the *Now!*

Toyota's two pillars, just-in-time and autonomation, differ from convenience stores in their time of arrival and in their approach. Yet they are similar in seeking to lead management into a new way of grappling with the *Now!*

What is *Now!* is both a philosophical and a very real question for people today. Looking ahead to the twenty-first century and a rapidly advancing Information Age, it is extremely important to find a way to grapple with and live in the *Now!*

▾

Dialogue A: An information system that provides exactly what is needed when it is needed

Mito: You have said that if Henry Ford were alive today he would produce a production system just like Toyota's. It must be then that his successors distorted his original intentions.

Ohno: Planned mass production, symbolized by the phrase "mass production, mass sales," brought unlimited material prosperity and gave rise to the American Century. Therefore, the entrepreneurs who used this system and those who studied it in business schools are totally entranced by its power.

During Japan's period of rapid growth from the late 1950s to the early 1970s, and in the United States since the end of the Great Depression, there has never been a sense of material scarcity. In fact, it has been an era of continuous prosperity. There have been peaks and valleys, but the general long-term trend has been towards increasing prosperity.

People end up taking such prosperity for granted. The entrepreneurs who should be sensitive to the fragility of prosperity and the university-trained professional managers came to believe that America's prosperity would continue forever.

Believing that "bigger is better," they increased the size of plants and facilities to giant proportions. Believing that "more is better," they strove to push production speed to the outer limits. Coupling mass production with America's specialty — mass sales — they became lost in a dream. They ignored the negative side of this policy — that "mass production, mass sales" is accompanied by many forms of waste.

Mito: The "planned" in "planned mass production" carried with it an ironic meaning. America also had been a place where anything produced could be sold. Production was based on the American idea of scientific control. They felt that their success was due to the power of American-style marketing, which analyzed diverse data gathered with sophisticated market research.

But we now realize that the magical American management and marketing were in fact ivory-tower theories producing outmoded management methods based on past information. As long as prosperity continued, the waste within the organizations remained hidden.

Ohno: A glance might enable us to see some waste scattered here and there. During the years of continuous prosperity, however, more than enough surplus profits offset that waste, making management indifferent to small amounts. In an absolute sense, however, those amounts were not small. Since the system was inherently flawed, they could not grasp to what a serious extent the waste really was.

Organizations like these were weakened by bureaucratic control. Carried away with prosperity, however, the managers could not see this reality at all. This was true of Japan as well in its period of rapid growth.

The eyes of Japanese managers were blinded by prosperity and unable to see the hidden danger. That which forced all managers, indeed everyone in the world, to pay attention to hidden waste was the first oil crisis in the fall of 1973. In that regard, the oil crisis was a revolutionary event globally. That year, the "bigger is better" way of thinking came to an end.

It was also the year Japan entered a new dimension. For the first time since its defeat in World War II, Japan had reached a mature and gradual economic growth.

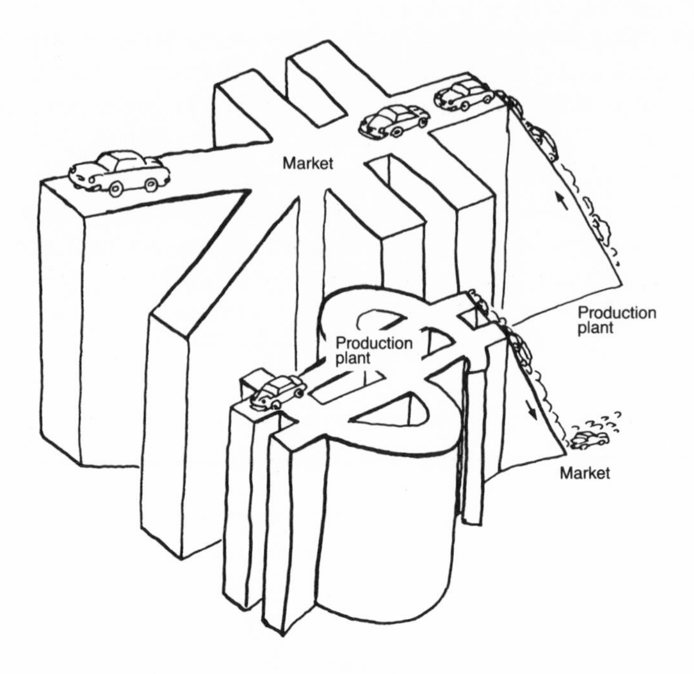

Figure 5. In the Toyota production system, the market *pulls* the needed goods. In the Ford system, the company forcefully *pushes* products on the market.

▸ Waste wreaks havoc to the extent that growth slows down

Mito: Entering a new dimension means that the rules and previously established order no longer apply. The "mass production, mass sales" system went bankrupt. The shock of the first oil crisis was enough to make the manufacturing industry reconsider its "big guns and warships" management philosophy and start to deal with its useless inventory-producing machines. It took pains to deal with the suddenly exposed waste and start looking in the direction of the Toyota production system. Oil prices had increased four or five times and more innovative thinking was demanded.

Ohno: There is a limit to the growth of all material things. Growth slows down, sometimes reversing itself. If mentally unprepared for this, we will be unable to deal with the situation when it occurs.

The Toyota production system strives to eliminate all waste because waste wreaks havoc when growth slows down or stops. In a period when anything made can be sold, useless inventory does not attract attention — but once growth drops, it shows.

As the name implies, useless inventory cannot be sold even at fire-sale prices. Useless work in process and finished goods lie idle in the warehouse while interest must be paid on the working capital. Any profits made are quickly consumed by the warehousing costs.

"Rationalization" means to get rid of fat. As they say, "an ounce of prevention is worth a pound of cure," but somehow people don't take this to heart. Only when they become overweight do they worry about keeping trim. And then, it's not easy.

Mito: The auto industry has its well-known Maxcy-Silberston curve. As the production system expands to meet rising demands, the cost curve moves in the opposite direction as average costs decrease. The Ford system was able to enjoy the fruits of this curve as long as the demand kept rising. Yet, as long as there are mountains, there must also be valleys — the demand for automobiles cannot rise forever.

When the demand starts to move back down the curve, the costs will increase as dramatically as they had decreased when moving up the curve. We can, in fact, draw a reverse Maxcy-Silberston curve.

There is a need for some sort of shock absorber to deal with decreases in demand. Since the Toyota production system is a mechanism for feeling even the smallest fluctuations in demand, it plays the role of just such a shock absorber.

Ohno: If the road is just a little rough, we can run along as usual without bumping too much. For a manager, however, there is nothing better than having a mechanism or shock absorber for dealing with changes in the external environment beyond his or her control. This is a fundamental aim of the Toyota production system.

On the surface, the economy appears to be running along smoothly. If we look at a graph of any given period of prosperity, it might be possible to imagine the future based on past trends. It is not enough, however, for managers of a private enterprise to rely on general trends. They must be aware of changes in market conditions. They must *feel* the sales fluctuations of their companies' products as they occur.

The Toyota production system allows managers to feel the competition in the marketplace and the pains of market changes. By feeling such changes, it is possible to formulate a response. To feel such pain is to witness the continuously fleeting moments of time and grasp the information from the absolute *Now!* Being able to grasp and effectively utilize such information is a key to management survival in the Information Age.

The relationship between action and time is elusive. Any action or information quickly becomes part of the past. To rely on such past information is to fail to grasp the essence of the *Now!* market and will lead to the production of a large mountain of unsold goods.

The Toyota production system responds just-in-time to the needs of the *Now!* market by providing exactly what is needed when it is needed. Putting aside for a moment the production plant, let's return to the example of the convenience store. It anticipates the Information Age. Positioned at the very nerve center of the marketplace, through its extensive POS system, the convenience store incorporates consumer needs as they arise.

Composed of strategic software and hardware, a POS system serves as a management information weapon in a fiercely competitive market. If managers have a penetrating mind and a sense of the times, they can grasp precisely the *Now!* and put the information to use to their hearts' content.

▸ The convenience store has penetrated the consumer mind

Mito: Itoh Masatoshi of Itoh Yokado is just such a manager. Two years after the first oil crisis, he visited you and left no doubt that he was quite inspired by the discussion.

Ten years later in November 1985, he introduced POS systems into every department of each store in the Itoh chain. As a first step into the Information Age, 8,000 POS registers were installed. With this system, Itoh Yokado is said to control all of its 600,000 items. This makes it possible to know instantaneously how much of which product is selling.

Within the Itoh Yokado Group, 7-Eleven Japan first introduced the POS system. Management decided on the system as an effective weapon to aid decisionmaking by providing *Now!* information. It took the lead in Japan's distribution industry by installing POS systems companywide beginning in September 1982. The ultimate decision, of course, was made by Mr. Itoh. It was Suzuki Toshifumi, President of 7-Eleven Japan, however, who took everything the American 7-Eleven had to offer and improved upon it to create a superior Japanese model.

In November 1973, immediately after the oil crisis, 7-Eleven Japan was established. Mr. Suzuki had visited the United States in the late 1960s and was apparently impressed with the appearance and atmosphere of the successful 7-Eleven chain of the Southland Corporation.

At first he was surprised to find that 7-Eleven stores operated 16 or 24 hours a day. Moreover, he was amazed to find that in the small space of 1,000 square feet individual stores managed over 3,000 items. He felt the convenience store was just as the name implied — convenient. From that point on, he began collecting and assimilating all the information needed to construct such a system in Japan — distribution, store construction, the flow and arrangement of goods, and sales.

Ohno: Every product or industry has a natural life. This knowledge may have directed Mr. Suzuki's thinking. That is to say, looking at the United States, perhaps he saw a trend from centralization to dispersion. The supermarket had become a mature industry — and new growth was in fast-food chains and convenience stores located closer to the consumers' homes.

▾

Dialogue B: Looking at America fires the imagination

Mito: Mr. Suzuki's process of conceptualization has much in common with your observations of U.S. supermarkets. He had contact with American convenience stores early on and was able to give full vent to his imagination. You, on the other hand, despite having fallen in love with the concept, were unable to visit a supermarket right away. Your imagination worked in unusual and interesting ways. By the time you actually saw a supermarket, you realized that what you previously had imagined to be a Toyota production system was actually a pseudo-Toyota Ohno system. From that realization the entire Toyota production system began to take shape.

It is a valuable case study to compare how your respective imaginations reacted to stimuli from the environment and developed your systems.

Ohno: As income rises, material needs are satisfied and leisure time and time at home increases. The trend, therefore, turns away from a system based on large mass-sales supermarkets to one based on convenience stores located closer to the customers' homes. Suzuki Toshifumi's foresight is demonstrated in his instant perception of this trend and his bringing of such enterprises to the Japanese market.

Mito: Your contribution was from the production plant floor where you created a production flow in order to eliminate waste. You did this by analyzing the relationships between workers, between machines, and between workers and machines. Ultimately, you found it impossible to eliminate all waste by dabbling in just one area of the plant.

You realized you would have to figure out how to respond quickly and accurately to the car dealers who were the actual source of information. This is where the diverse consumers come to purchase the particular car they want. As a manufacturer, you grappled with the theme of providing the market with exactly what it needed when it needed it. Changing the main point of reference from the production plant to the marketplace was quite an innovation.

Ohno: Indeed it was revolutionary. Reflecting on industrial history in Japan since the Meiji Restoration (1867–1912), we find the underlying current has been material scarcity. Therefore, the categorical imperative on the national, company, and

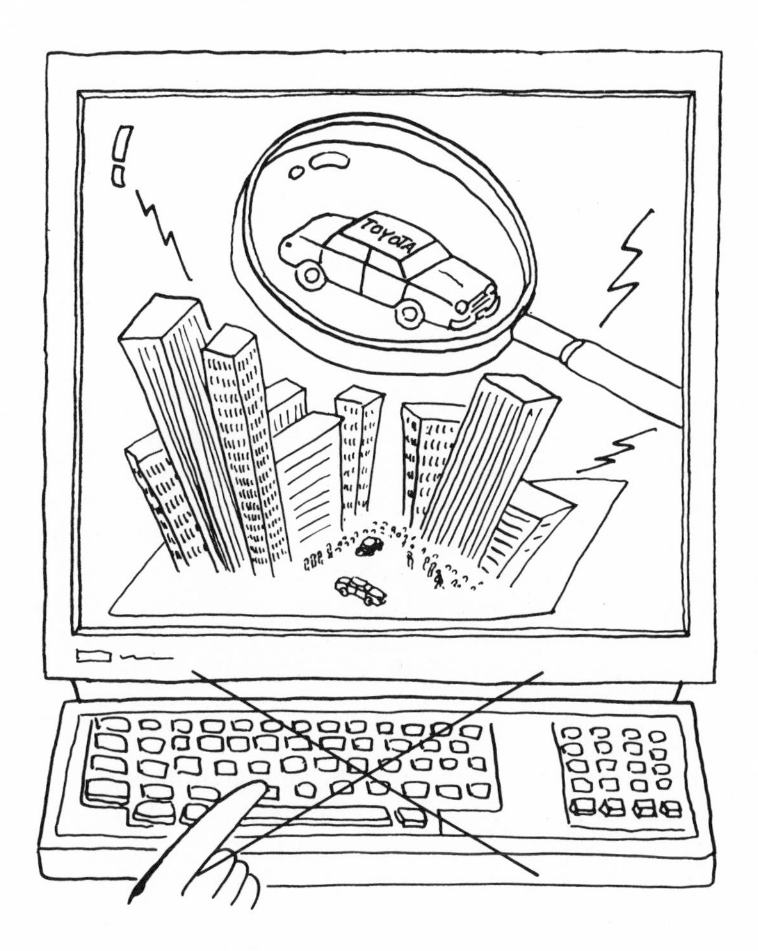

Figure 6. The source of information is already in the market. We simply must stand there and observe.

individual level has been to produce things as rapidly as possible. The ingrained way of thinking among entrepreneurs — manufacturers in particular — was to produce rapidly and to produce a lot. Whatever was made could be sold.

Japan's manufacturing advanced rapidly in the postwar era. The 1960s marked its first experience with material prosperity. One would expect managers to lose their bearings in this new environment. No one had dared expect such a long period of peace and prosperity. On the industrial front, existing thinking was not enough to respond to the changed environment. The main change was that one could not grasp the basic manufacturing issues and address them directly without focusing on the marketplace.

Mr. Suzuki's changes in the distribution and retailing business were revolutionary. Because, however, he was not in manufacturing, he naturally encountered resistance.

▸ The foresight and imagination of Suzuki Toshifumi

Mito: When speaking with Mr. Suzuki, I found it most interesting that while in the process of visiting American convenience stores he had never heard of the Toyota production system. At that time, companies in secondary industries only knew that Toyota seemed to be doing something unusual. To those in tertiary industries, the system was unknown.

You spoke of Mr. Suzuki's actions as revolutionary. In that respect, you two have something in common. You saw Toyota grow into a mammoth organization insensitive to the feelings of individual consumers. Mr. Suzuki realized the same thing about supermarkets.

Itoh Yokado also grew rapidly, becoming more bureaucratic. Essential information failed to be delivered at the needed times. Both of you realized the importance of looking at business from a market viewpoint and broke away from the current thinking. These similarities occurred even though the two of you worked in different environments.

Ohno: It does seem that as supermarkets evolved from groups of individual stores into nationwide chains that the "bigger is better" syndrome crept into current thinking. Retailing's key function, purchasing, became centralized. From that point on, it became difficult to escape the vicious spiral of "mass production, mass purchasing, mass sales." This is the same "big guns and warships" pattern we saw in the automobile industry under the Ford system.

Suzuki Toshifumi recognized that "big guns and warships" could not grasp individual consumer needs and created too much waste in the supermarket system. He foresaw the entry of smaller stores into the neighborhoods where consumers actually lived.

I dislike "big guns and warships" for the same reason. In the production plant, we must respond personally to individual orders.

▸ Human tenacity in pursuit of a complete system

Mito: Itoh Masatoshi saw the necessity of changing the retailing business. Following the first oil crisis, he went in search of a new system and saw the Toyota production system as a possible answer. Meanwhile Mr. Suzuki, his trusted subordinate, was traveling both inside and outside Japan developing new ideas. As a result, he reached an agreement with the Southland Corporation and 7-Eleven of the United States.

In certain respects, Mr. Itoh and Mr. Suzuki's relationship is comparable to that of yourself with Toyoda Eiji. At first the Toyota production system was not widely accepted in the company and for many years was repulsed as an "Ohno system." Of course, Mr. Suzuki did not encounter such resistance in implementing his plans with 7-Eleven. The similarity is that you both were trusted by your superiors and encouraged to develop your ideas into a company system. Isn't it true?

Ohno: It is true with all projects that without the trust of your superiors you cannot succeed. Toyoda Eiji and Saitō Naoichi were my two superiors at this time. No matter how much criticism the system received, never once did they say "Stop!" Best of all, they quietly supported me along the way.

This relationship of trust with my superiors was unflinching. I never heard a word of criticism from outside the department: they took it all for me and never passed it on. Itoh Masatoshi and Suzuki Toshifumi likewise had a mutual trust that allowed Mr. Suzuki to carry out his plans.

Mito: A relationship based on trust gives birth to a perseverance that blossoms when it encounters a crisis.

For example, Mr. Suzuki was absorbed in the convenience store project when the first oil crisis hit. He viewed it as an opportunity to rejuvenate the company. Considering his tenacity, we realize that this was not only natural but almost inevitable. His meticulous planning and preparation created new opportunities for him to take decisive action.

Ohno: Human foresight and insight come from understanding social changes. Mr. Suzuki ably demonstrated this understanding through his work. His success was no accident.

Mito: You and Mr. Suzuki are similar in that regard. Individuals with foresight seize upon the signs of change and act upon them immediately. This ability is clear when change occurs. Although it may appear that success is due to chance, for certain individuals change is chance, meaning that any change can be an opportunity for success.

Mr. Suzuki knew prior to the oil crisis that consumers' values were changing and tastes were becoming more diverse. What had been thought of as "the public" was splintering in different directions. The ensuing economic crisis made this obvious.

In a mature economy, the compact, decentralized convenience chains should be more suitable than large, centralized supermarkets. Therefore it was extremely opportune that 7-Eleven emerged on the scene when it did. Founded as York Seven, the chain was renamed 7-Eleven in January 1978.

Ohno: Putting it that way fires my imagination. On the one hand, Mr. Itoh took a scalpel to the huge organization and made structural changes. Meanwhile Mr. Suzuki started with what we might call the blank canvas of the Japanese archipelago and made it his goal to paint a 7-Eleven in every corner of the picture.

▸ Information is the password to the future

Mito: Suzuki Toshifumi made quite an achievement in establishing convenience stores throughout Japan. In the franchise-chain system, the headquarters — in this case, 7-Eleven Japan — provides various kinds of know-how and assistance to the individual affiliated stores. In exchange for this know-how and support, sales profits are divided between headquarters and the stores — 45 percent for headquarters, 55 percent for the affiliate. This is a rational system. It gives the headquarters the resources with which to develop the software necessary to enter the Information Age.

This system of franchising convenience stores has brought both the distribution and information revolutions not only to industry but to all of society. What you are doing in Toyota plants, making individual products for individual consumers — first got its start in the various 7-Eleven stores. In the small space of 1,000 square feet, over 3,000 different items are constantly turned over.

In this system, just as in the Toyota production system, small lots and "leveled" thinking are indispensable. In developing this system, it is necessary to break away from using traditional wholesalers who only cover their own territories. We must not be confined by the old system, but must encourage the development of a new breed of wholesalers — vendors who will deliver directly to the retail outlet.

In order to construct a convenience store system, we must be able to do several things. We must have a fixed set of items deliverable on schedule in the appropriate quantities to the various stores in the chain. Because Mr. Suzuki saw the necessity of breaking away from the traditional way of doing things, he met with great resistance at first, just as you did.

Nevertheless, this resistance was overcome because of the overriding economic and social advantages offered by the convenience stores. The possibilities created by the ability to master the flow of information are limitless.

Ohno: There is, of course, the benefit of extended hours of operation, which provides convenience to the consumer. Then there is the constant turnover of different products which makes goods available that the consumer wants and removes those no longer desired. This has been one of the main forces behind the growth of convenience stores.

The turnover of goods is in fact driven by the turnover of information. A principle tool enabling 7-Eleven to capture this information was the POS system.

▸ Can you grasp the *Now!*?

Mito: 7-Eleven took advantage of the convergence of computers and communications early on. Recognizing the value of this development, managers use POS to achieve the maximum utility from available store space. It has become a management tool that fully utilizes all information.

In the POS system, each time something is entered on the store's cash register, the item, number, time, and price is transmitted to the home computer. The home computer analyzes this information, enabling management to develop product, purchasing, and delivery strategies for maximum total effect. In the Information Age, this is the goal towards which all companies strive.

Suzuki Toshifumi's insight was in realizing our need to solve an apparent contradiction. Most information traditionally received by management was already part of the past. *Now!* information is scarce indeed.

Ohno: That's a good point. I have often criticized the Ford system for this reason. The marketing elite from headquarters often uses old information to develop the ivory-tower plans they unilaterally impose on the plant floor. This leads to the production of mountains of useless inventory.

"What is *Now!*?" sounds like a philosophical question — but it really isn't. We ultimately are asking how the production plant is going to respond quickly to individual orders for products originating in the marketplace.

Take, for example, the customer who enters a bakery and orders ten cookies. That order for ten is the *Now!* information. Many different cookies are kept in stock. Twenty or 30 of each kind are made based on previous sales trends with the possibility that some will not sell. There is also the chance that the bakery will not have in stock what the customer wants, making it better to bake ten cookies when you get the order. *Produce only what is needed when it is needed in the amount needed.* This is the heart of just-in-time. However, it is easier in theory than in practice.

At this point, you begin wondering how best to grasp the *Now!* The Ford system, no matter how you look at it, is based on the past. When I was pondering this point, it occurred to me that the secret was somehow hidden in the design of the American supermarket.

Ultimately, the development of the Toyota production system was the pursuit of the *Now!* information before it became part of the past. It may indeed be possible now to give consumers exactly what they want when they want it.

Competition among companies in a free marketplace will become more severe as sellers bend over backwards to please the customer. But it makes no sense to sell at a loss. The only solution is to cut costs to maintain profits at a lower price.

Today, information systems will be the point of competition among companies. Whoever can best grasp and utilize *Now!* information will win.

▸ Unsalability is more important than salability

Mito: I find it interesting that Mr. Suzuki says a 7-Eleven will not be a store of best sellers. One would think a storekeeper would want to keep popular items in stock and give them additional shelf space. Retailing has always pursued this type of salability.

However, this is also the path to mountains of unsold inventory and reliance on past information. Mr. Suzuki rejected this method. It would not be the same 7-Eleven if he did otherwise. He saw the opportunity to rely on unsalability rather than salability.

In other words, salability information is valuable when developing new products and improving old ones. However, to produce new products one after another based on past trends is no longer rooted in the present. To that end, emphasis must be on unsalability. We must constantly remove products that are not selling to create space on the shelves. You can rotate this now available space between the new and improved prod-

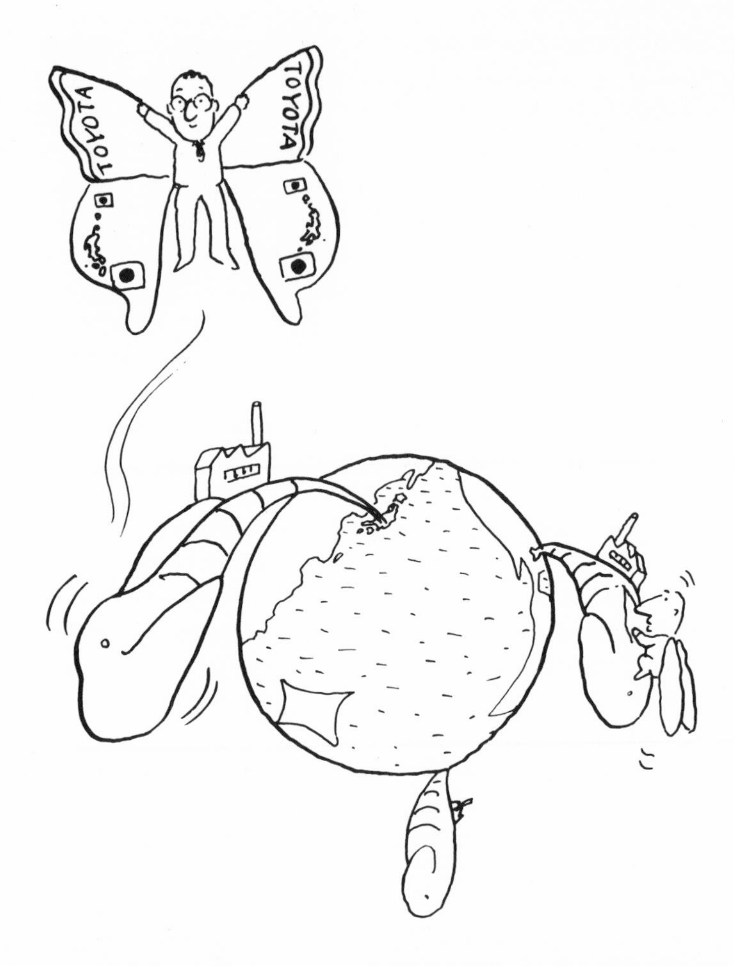

Figure 7. Management systems that transcend national and all other borders.

ucts based on salability. By constantly removing those products demonstrating unsalability, we create a *Now!* situation. Putting new products on empty shelves is an act that goes beyond the present to the future. Thus we see how 7-Eleven's have no connection at all with past information.

Ohno: When selling thousands of items to many, diverse consumers, it is not easy to see the whole picture. It is easier to focus on unsalability by removing non-selling products and rotating newly developed products on the shelves. This way we can be in touch with the *Now!* information continuously and provide exactly what is needed, when needed, in the quantities needed.

▸ Don't drown in computer hardware

Mito: The 7-Eleven system makes the most of human intelligence. It is a powerful concept that removes non-selling products in order to grasp current information and give life to the shelf space.

These days, POS systems are popular in all companies and industries because of the spread of personal computers and the accelerated connection between computers and telecommunications. Seven-Eleven has taken advantage of all the latest information-processing machines, office automation equipment, and various computer terminals. Although the system is a product of all this hardware, the key is really the unique software 7-Eleven uses to run the system. Anyone can buy hardware but without software, it will be useless.

Some people say, irrationally, that the Toyota production system is outdated because it uses little scraps of paper (kanban) instead of sophisticated computers that enable you to transmit information instantly from a keyboard.

Ohno: I don't oppose introducing personal computers or other terminals into the factory. But to forget the original purpose of kanban and ridicule the scraps of paper invites a terrible result.

Using the keyboard of a personal computer to say "Give me this much of that at this time" simply plays the same role of kanban. The issue is knowing what the advantage is. There is no merit in excessively fast transmission of information. The essence of the Toyota production system is just-in-time. To transmit information too fast invites overproduction and its wastes.

These little scraps of paper, on the other hand, check overproduction. Furthermore, they prevent producing defective goods, concealing problems, and help control inventory. Of course, the personal computer is amazing as a product of modern civilization. But its true value in the production plant will be demonstrated only when combined with extensive telecommunications networks.

Mito: As you suggest, as it enters the Information Age, Japan suffers from an imbalance between hardware and software. This lag in software development is especially clear in comparison to America. For example, the United States is ahead in Information Networking Systems (INS), Value-Added Networks (VAN), Local Area Networks (LAN), and Cable Television (CATV), among others. As information is able to transcend national borders via space satellites, these systems have great significance.

However, in facing the Information Age, we must realize that even a scrap of paper is superior to a computer if the computer is not used intelligently. The scrap of paper is, in fact, information and mental software.

Merely installing a personal computer in every home and establishing a telecommunications network will not be enough. Creating a flow of information will not even be enough. Money and goods must flow through this network as well. We must be able to place an order on the keyboard and arrange for the transfer of funds and home delivery of the product. The Toyota production system is an advanced information system. When given strategic software, it will blossom and achieve success as a management system of the Information Age.

▼

Mito's Commentary

▸ Studying Henry Ford's awareness of time and waste, we realize that were he alive today he would do the same as Taiichi Ohno

Taiichi Ohno believes that were Henry Ford alive today, they would both be creating the same kind of system. He argues that Mr. Ford had a keen awareness of time and waste.

The following is a passage from Henry Ford's book, *Today and Tomorrow*, first published in 1926:

> The time element in manufacturing stretches from the moment the raw material is separated from the earth to the moment when the finished product is delivered to the ultimate consumer. It involves all forms of transportation and has to be considered in every national scheme of service. It is a method of saving and serving which ranks with the application of power and the division of labor.
>
> If we were operating today under the methods of 1921, we should have on hand raw materials to the value of about one hundred and twenty million dollars, and we should have unnecessarily in transit finished products to the value of about fifty million dollars. Instead of that, we have an average investment of only about fifty million dollars, or, to put it another way, our inventory, raw and finished, is less than it was when our production was only half as great.
>
> The extension of our business since 1921 has been very great, yet, in a way, all this great expansion has been paid for out of money which, under our old methods, would have lain idle in piles of iron, steel, coal, or in finished automobiles stored in warehouses. We do not own or use a single warehouse![1]

It's amazing that even in the 1920s this kind of thinking was going on in the implementation of the Ford system. "For the masses" was the principle of this thoroughly rational system. Its goal was the total elimination of waste. The following words of Ford come straight from the heart of an entrepreneur:

> Hiring two men to do the job of one is a crime against society. Also, to carry a product 500 miles to the consumer, if that product can be found within 250 miles, is a crime. For a railroad to deliver in ten days when it might deliver in five is grand larceny.[2]

We find the essence of his thinking about wasting time in the following excerpt:

> It is not possible to repeat too often that waste is not something which comes after the fact. Restoring an ill body to health is an achievement, but preventing illness is a much higher achievement. Picking up and reclaiming the scrap left over after produc-

tion is a public service, but planning so that there will be no scrap is a higher public service.

Time waste differs from material waste in that there can be no salvage. The easiest of all wastes, and the hardest to correct, is this waste of time, because wasted time does not litter the floor like wasted material. In our industries, we think of time as human energy. If we buy more material than we need for production, then we are storing human energy — and probably depreciating its value. One may buy ahead on speculation in the hope of realizing an unearned profit. That is both poor service and poor business, because, over a term of years, the profits of speculation will not exceed the losses, and the net result to the speculator is zero, while the community itself has lost by having to make detours from the ordinary highways of trade.[3]

We see the "superrationalism" underlying Henry Ford's entrepreneurial spirit. Mr. Ford once scolded his financial officer for not considering the cost of products that couldn't be sold. His argument is convincing.

▸ Had Henry Ford and Alfred P. Sloan met in competition, perhaps the outcome would have been an American-style Toyota system

From 1924 to 1926 the American automobile market underwent a revolutionary change. Since the introduction of the Model T in 1908, luxury cars had been designed for a limited set of consumers. At a stroke, however, luxury cars were no longer a limited commodity but available to the public as well.

The market changed. Mr. Ford's concept of the automobile as a cheap mode of transportation evolved into Alfred P. Sloan's (1875–1966) idea that cars for the general public would improve continuously. The following comments are from Mr. Sloan's book, *My Years with General Motors*:

In the 1920s the American economy began a new period of expansion. Along with this came new phenomena and the market changed from what it had been in the past. It was a turning point for the automobile industry.

> These changes can be broken into four categories. One, the introduction of installment plan sales. Two, the trade-in of used cars. Three, the advent of the sedan. Four, the appearance of annual models. (If we include changes in the environment for the automobile we must add the improvement of the public roads.) These changes now have deep roots in the automobile industry. It is impossible to avoid consideration of them.
>
> Before 1920 and for a short time thereafter, the purchaser of an automobile was a first-time buyer and usually paid in cash. He bought either a roadster or a touring car, and the model did not differ from the year before and did not seem as though it would change in the future. These conditions continued for a while and, even if there was a change, it was nothing climactic. Each of the changes occurred separately and at its own pace, until one day we realized that there had been a revolution in the marketplace.[4]

Alfred Sloan was suggesting that the Model T was out of date because customers desired newer and more luxurious automobiles. This new era did not pass unnoticed. Mr. Sloan immediately organized GM strategy around a full-line policy. In today's language, he foresaw the diversification of the marketplace. Entrepreneurial businesspeople must see this diversification and develop a strategy of segmentation.

However, we can find no evidence that he developed a new GM production system corresponding to his new strategy of the full-line policy. Nevertheless, his insight was brilliant. He foresaw that which was to come in the near future: the birth and exploding growth of the consumer society.

In his book *The Americans: The Democratic Experience*, Daniel J. Boorstin gives a full account of American consumer society. He describes how Sloan the manufacturer, by introducing a new automobile model yearly, turned interest toward the consumer.

> This was the annual model. The spirit and purpose of the annual model were, of course, quite opposite to those of Ford and his Model T. "The great problem of the future," Sloan wrote to Lawrence P. Fisher, maker of Fisher Bodies, on September 9, 1927, "is to have our cars different from each other and different from year to year." The annual model, then, was part of a purposeful, planned program. And it was based on creating expectations of marvelous, if usually vague, novelties-always-to-come.

> Sloan and his able collaborators at General Motors set up a styling department (which by 1963 would employ more than fourteen hundred workers). They showed a concern for color, they "invented" new colors, and gave aphrodisiac names to old colors. Now for the first time their automobile designers included women. "It is not too much to say," Sloan explained, "that the 'laws' of the Paris dressmakers have come to be a factor in the automobile industry — and woe to the company which ignores them."[5]

Mr. Sloan's entrepreneurial spirit was in no way inferior to his rival's. By capitalizing on the diversification of the market, with his wide variation strategy he was able to overpower Henry Ford and achieve great success. Yet with such an extreme emphasis on the marketplace, he failed to devote sufficient time to rationalizing his production system. Because of this lack of competition, the Ford system, its hidden defects aside, became more deeply rooted in the American auto industry.

In stronger words, Alfred Sloan incurred high costs both in losses and waste to produce a very ostentatious Cadillac just to upstage the Model T. To cover himself, he charged a very high price.

In the 1960s and 1970s, as external labor-union problems compounded the many internal problems of the production plant, the American automobile industry fell apart. While a decisive and thorough management revolution is going on, the 1980s find the unions beginning to adjust their attitudes.

Did Henry Ford's sense of time and awareness of waste really get to the heart of the matter? And just how insightful were Mr. Sloan's ideas of diversification and segmentation? It seems that the Toyota production system is the best of both worlds.

▸ *Sooner or later, all growth levels off.* While an economist may concur with this statement, managers of private enterprises must continue to seek ways to create new growth opportunities

All real growth is structural. The interrelationship of the elements of such growth changes and becomes more complex over time.

Insofar as all organizations are living things, they are growing. For growth to continue, regeneration is indispensable. Fresh air is needed. New strengths will come forward and replace the old. The forces of positive and negative growth will collide and ultimately result in harmony. An organization's form and essence can regenerate itself completely within five or ten years.

The Toyota production system gives the impression of being a "hard" system promoting a concrete, fixed way of doing things in its pursuit of mechanizing, automating, and rationalizing the production plant. As a management system, however, Toyota has left that dimension behind. Taiichi Ohno accepts the challenge of helping organizations regenerate themselves because he recognizes that growth is limited. This is why the Toyota system, as a system, should be "soft" — not hard.

▸ The dispersal of production leveling marked the end of the Maxcy-Silberston curve. Toyota's production system was best suited to soften the shock of its reversal

The Maxcy-Silberston curve is the concept of economies of scale that resulted from the research of the English economists Aubrey Silverston of Cambridge University and George Maxcy of Hull University. Their book *The Motor Industry*, published in 1959, presents the results of years of detailed analysis of the special characteristics of the British automobile industry.

The researchers asked what the impact was on the cost per unit when production quantities leapt from 100,000 to 200,000 units, and then to 300,000 and 400,000. The response from the automobile manufacturers was conservative. They said volumes initially doubled while total cost per unit declined 8 percent. When volume doubled the second time, however, total cost declined 5 percent. When questioned about manufacturing cost rather than total cost per unit, the decreases were even greater. They discovered that a manufacturer with a present production level of 100,000 units contemplating an increase to 400,000 units could expect a reduction of 25 percent of the controllable costs, or about 15 percent of the total cost of the automobile.

This research was done in England over a quarter of a century ago. Yet the concepts have been used and popularized in the belief that the percentage of profits increases with volume. The Maxcy-Silberston curve, in fact, became an index for all subsequent automobile manufacturers. So too did the idea that profits would decrease as volume decreased, as was the case in several recessions.

This fear was experienced following the 1973 oil crisis when Japan experienced its 1974 zero growth. The automobile industry could not escape the effects of the crisis. Restrictive laws on gasoline were passed, and the consumer movement to conserve gasoline made matters worse. Only through emphasis on total quality control (TQC) and the resultant increase of exports to America was the Japanese economy able to recover. It is safe to say that the oil crisis made a deep impact on the mind of every manager in Japan.

A concrete example of this was the rapid diffusion of the Toyota production system immediately after the oil crisis. Manufacturing firms involved in the automobile industry experienced a tremendous shock when they suddenly found themselves on a reverse Maxcy-Silberston curve.

In fact, from this point on, the Toyota production system began spreading to other industries as well. Until then most companies had indulged themselves because they could sell anything they made. They were disinclined to listen to the diverse needs of their customers. They soon realized, however, the impossibility of increasing profits because the production gains dictated by the Maxcy-Silberston curve were not materializing.

In this respect, this curve and all the other logical extensions of the Ford "bigger is better," "planned mass production" system became myths.

▸ The old-fashioned neighborhood grocery is today the convenience store with 7-Eleven Japan's Suzuki Toshifumi at the forefront. We cannot discuss the distribution industry the way we can operations such as steel, automobiles, and paper pulp. Lying somewhere between capital and human logic, distribution is a marginal industry some think should do no further industrialization

The above words are from Tsutsumi Seiji (1927–) leader of the Seibu Seven Group.

To expand a little, the distribution industry is viewed from many non-economic perspectives, including political, social, and cultural. The industry itself believes it constantly must strive to modernize to keep up with the desires of its many consumers — "modernize" meaning capital logic or capital intensive. Necessarily, as the industry has modernized, it has accelerated the urbanization trend throughout the Japanese archipelago, changing the residential environment of many communities.

In other words, the supermarket, empowered with capital logic, has developed through the maximum use of land and labor, revolutionizing the distribution industry. But its excessive enthusiasm in fulfilling consumer's material needs has also disrupted the traditional landscape of many small retailers in the typical community. Mr. Tsutsumi currently is examining his company's impact on these developments.

How should the distribution industry modernize without destroying the traditional balance between history, culture, and business? The best qualified to be called a success in this struggle is the convenience store (CVS). The leader in this field is 7-Eleven Japan, spearheaded by Mr. Suzuki.

When 7-Eleven Japan was born, in the midst of the first oil crisis, Mr. Suzuki already had perceived that the development of mass retail outlets would peak with the maturity of the consumer market. He saw retailing's need to get much closer to the consumer's home. He began investigating the American model.

In 1971 he visited Southland corporate headquarters in Dallas, Texas, to began negotiations. When deciding whether or not there was in fact a need for convenience stores in Japan, he was struck most by the fact that conveniences for daily living were not keeping pace with advances in material prosperity.

For example, even though the trends toward a 24-hour city and the late-night family in which family members work, study, or play late at night were continuing, there were no signs of late-night stores in the neighborhoods. People's only choice was to make instant noodles at home. But it was not just the needs of the late-night consumer that were unsatisfied. He saw the time had come in Japan when consumers would appreciate the convenience offered by 7-Eleven in the morning, daytime, and evening. This just happened to coincide with the 1973 oil crisis.

The system that absorbs the "pains" of market changes

Mr. Suzuki and his staff devoted themselves to becoming masters of the franchise chain (FC) system. Their biggest challenge was developing a backup system to educate and strengthen the various stores, some of which are owned by headquarters and others by affiliated owners. Mr. Suzuki and his team met that challenge successfully.

To provide for the extended hours of year-round operation, work schedules of the owners, employees, and part-timers had to be arranged meticulously and various issues dealt with individually. For instance:

- How to manage the arrangement and delivery of 3,000 items.
- How to negotiate purchase prices that are less than a supermarket pays.
- How to share profits between headquarters and affiliate stores.
- How to appeal to neighborhood residents.
- What should be the advertising strategy.

1. **Visiting Prospective Owners**

   A recruiting field counselor (RFC) visits an area where a new affiliate store is desired. Candidates are interviewed to see if they can fulfill the conditions required for operating a 7-Eleven.

2. **Market Research**

   Market conditions of the prospective location are observed from different angles and the data analyzed.

3. **Information about the 7-Eleven System**

   The philosophy and details for operation and management of a 7-Eleven store are explained until the prospective owner understands and consents.

4. **Explaining the Franchise Contact**

   The contract is explained carefully.

5. **Signing the Franchise Contract**

   Following explanation and consideration, the contract is signed.

6. **Store Planning and Design**

   The design department undertakes the layout of a functional store that is easy to work in and, of course, easy to buy in. The customer path, proper temperature and lighting, and efficiency in everything from equipment to maintenance is considered.

7. **Signing the Construction Contract**

   An architect and construction company are brought in and a contract signed.

8. **Preparation for Opening**

   Construction is carried out. Display stands stipulated in the design are ordered and installed. Various manuals are delivered. Opening preparations begin to accelerate.

9. **Owner Education and Training**

   The new owner receives ten days of training required to run the store, including the operation of the computer system.

10. **Delivery and Display of Products prior to Opening**

    Products and vendors are selected with the advice of the RFC. Efficient delivery and product display is arranged prior to opening.

11. **"Turn-key"**

    When preparations are complete for the store to open the following day, the cash register key is handed over ceremoniously to the new owner. The RFC steps back, passing the baton to the operation field counselor (OFC).

(Continued on next page)

12. **Opening**

    The opening is announced in the local newspaper and through distribution of flyers.

13. **Operation of the 7-Eleven System**

    The point-of-sale (POS) system transmits information on the activity of products and customers. Another system arranges for the purchase and delivery of products. This unique combination of hardware and software supports the store owner.

14. **Management Consulting Visits by the OFC**

    The OFC, familiar with both the 7-Eleven system and the marketplace, visits the new owner at least twice a week and serves as a pipeline for information and analysis from the network of stores linked through headquarters.

Table 3. 7-Eleven Japan's 14 Steps from Contract to Store Opening

"Management's strength is in its systematization. Because it is essential to gain acceptance from and an in-depth understanding of the consumer, the convenience store must fundamentally be a place run by and for people."

This was Mr. Suzuki's management vision. He wanted to create a convenience store that would feel pain with market changes. This management strategy is equivalent to the Toyota production system: provide what is needed when it is needed and in the quantities needed. Mr. Ohno developed his system on the plant floor; Mr. Suzuki stood in the marketplace. Yet the ideas of both are merging with an impact stimulating to the entire world of industry.

7-Eleven, the information store

POS systems were installed in 7-Eleven Japan's stores beginning in September 1982. The storekeeper inputs the item and quantity bought, the other products with which it was bought, and what kind of customer made the purchase. This data is assembled and analyzed at headquarters.

The winter 1985 edition of the *Itoh Yokado Quarterly* reported that "in this manner, we are able to computerize the management of over 5,000 items. Analyzing sales trends can help us better understand salability and unsalability to come up with the following product strategies..."

The introduction of POS systems in Japan marked a new era and the development of new dimensions in POS technology. POS innovations as of 1985 are as follows:

1. Data entry people with the ability to process ten times more information five times faster.
2. Equipment for graphic display of information in the stores.
3. Presentations of real-time graphics made possible by the combination of data entry people and graphic display equipment.
4. The increased technical ability to transmit information, giving stores an almost instantaneous understanding of market trends.
5. Capabilities to accommodate those products not easily computer coded (soft drinks, for example). These products can be entered now with special keys and codes allowing management to collect yet another kind of data.

These simple, flexible management software systems respond to changing market conditions and complement the advanced hardware already installed. With the "informationization" of the stores, Mr. Suzuki sought to achieve his goal of humanizing 7-Eleven. He, better than anyone, has understood exactly what the market *Now!* is and has used this information to his advantage.

Retailing has been successfully modernized by 7-Eleven without destorying the traditional balance between history, culture, and commerce. In January 1986, there were 2,604 7-Eleven stores in Japan. There were also 1,178 Lawson stores of the Daiei Chain and 708 Familymart stores of the Seibu Seven Group.

- Mutual trust is best connected with an invisible thread. The relationships between Toyoda Eiji and Taiichi Ohno and that between Itoh Masatoshi and Suzuki Toshifumi approach this ideal

Max Picard, in his book *The World of Silence,*[6] says that silence is neither negative nor inexplicable. Rather, silence is a positive phenomenon existing independently in the world order. These are the very philosophical words of a philosopher, and they are mentioned here because they explain a lot about the activities of Taiichi Ohno within Toyota.

In the spring of 1932, in the midst of the Great Depression, Taiichi Ohno graduated from the mechanical engineering department of Nagoya High School and joined Toyoda Spinning and Weaving. He started off in textiles but was transferred to Toyota Motors in 1943. After the war, he remained in the automobile company. He was impressed by Toyoda Kiichirō's just-in-time idea and inspired by the inventive genius of the founder Toyoda Sakichi. His own contribution was in the field of autonomation. Still in his thirties and full of energy, Mr. Ohno set out to develop an Ohno system to challenge the Ford system.

His career and influence advanced rapidly. In 1947, at age 33, he was put in charge of the main factory in the general assembly division at headquarters. In 1948 he became responsible for the No. 2 machining facility at the Koromo plant. In 1949 he was made machine shop manager. In 1953 he was second in charge of manufacturing and promoted to a company director. Throughout this period, he was given more and more freedom to experiment with just-in-time methods.

His efforts aroused opposition. He tried a "supermarket system" in 1953. To create a production flow, he rearranged equipment on the floor and connected the assembly plant to the body plant. He strove to implement visual control. These measures were revolutionary compared to existing operations.

They refuted the existing conventions in manufacturing and wounded the pride of many. Anger was directed not so much at Mr. Ohno himself but at his superiors. He would not agree, as the Ford system dictated, that the bigger the lot size, the better, and that they should try to limit the number of die changes. Indeed, it would be unusual had there been no opposition from those in manufacturing.

Throughout his 35 years at Toyota, Mr. Ohno's superiors were Toyoda Eiji, currently chairman, and Saitō Naichi. They absorbed all the discontent and grumbling directed at Mr. Ohno from the factory and never mentioned it to him. They only wanted him to continue finding ways to reduce manufacturing costs. These men were bound together by an invisible thread of mutual trust, which brings to mind earlier words...

Reflecting on the past, Taiichi Ohno says:

> I knew all too well how they worried about me and what I was doing. Yet they never said "Do this!" or "Do that!" For my part, I never had to say "I'd like to do this" or "Please let me do that." I just did everything I thought had to be done. Had I asked permission, my resolve would have weakened because of the pressure to prove what I was doing. Had either side said anything, the relationship would have collapsed.

Max Picard says something similar when he notes that in the realm of silence, rather than us gazing at silence, silence watches us. In the same way, Itoh Masatoshi's relationship with Suzuki Toshifumi is supported by this silent thread.

▸ The Toyota information system underlies the Toyota production system. As we enter the Information Age, it will demonstrate not only refinement but tremendous development as well

The just-in-time system of providing exactly what is need in the quantity and at the time needed is an essential element of the Toyota production system. This applies not only to hardware such as automobiles and parts but to the software of information as well.

In fact, Toyota's information system is integral to its production system. Mr. Ohno gives an overview of this arrangement.

> First, the Toyota Motor Company has an annual plan. This means the rough number of cars — for instance, two million — to be produced and sold during the current year.
>
> Next, there is the monthly production schedule. For example, the type and quantities of cars to be made in March are announced internally early on and in February a more detailed schedule is "set." Both schedules are sent to the outside cooperating firms as they are developed. Based on these plans, the daily production schedule is established in detail and includes production leveling.
>
> In the Toyota production system, the method of setting up this daily schedule is important. During the last half of the previous month, each production line is informed of the daily production quantity for each product type. At Toyota, this is called the daily level. On the other hand, the daily sequence schedule is sent only to one place — the final assembly line. This is a special characteristic of Toyota's information system. In other companies, scheduling information is sent to every production process.
>
> This is how the Toyota information system works in production: when the production line workers use parts at the side of the line for assembly, they remove the kanban. The preceding process makes as many parts as were used, eliminating the need for a special production schedule. In other words, the kanban acts as a production order for the earlier processes.[7]

The main — as well as unique — feature of the Toyota information system is that it determines what is the *Now!* information. By trying not to send excess information, it prevents waste arising from overproduction. At the same time, it avoids the confusion that results in other firms when production plans are changed.

As we proceed into the Information Age, Toyota will take advantage of the convergence between computers and telecommunications to produce an even more refined Toyota information system. Furthermore, the progression toward an information network will accelerate with Toyota at the center and include all the factories, dealers, affiliated companies, and parts suppliers. We plan to develop a global Toyota information system to match the times.

3

Leadership Imagination and Decisiveness in the Information Age

Theme: Workplace management means approaching and eventually becoming the source of information

The word "workplace" constantly appears in statements such as: "He's just a head office big shot who knows nothing about the workplace" and "Management can't operate without an understanding of the workplace." We have been deluged by this word to the extent that we might wish to inquire where exactly is the workplace?

It goes without saying that for company presidents, the head office is a vital workplace for management activities. In this case, the workplace can be formal board meetings, informal discussions with executives and managers, as well as opportunities to interact with new employees. However, if the presidents isolate themselves in, say, their downtown offices, they will fail to stay informed about front-line, or workplace, conditions. This will hamper their ability for effective decisionmaking. In this case, the term "workplace" refers to the production plant where a company's products are manufactured or the forefront of the marketplace where products are sold.

At this point, once again I would like to ask the question, "Where exactly is the workplace?" It is not a mistake to say that production plants and retail stores are typical workplaces. Yet originally "workplace" was a more general term. Therefore, we must approach it realistically.

Searching for the workplace is an essential factor in defining the term. Perhaps we should define workplace as the necessary source of information, or the point closest to that source.

Japanese managers frequently allude to "workplace management." They have definitely attended to this area more so than their Western counterparts.

Since the Meiji period, industrialized Japan has experienced a history of confrontations between capital and labor and has been filled with acrimonious ideological conflicts. However, as the historical and traditional concepts of clanship and family have merged, Japan's industrialism and industrial organizations have developed along the lines of "family-style management." Even the three long-standing distinctive characteristics of Japanese management:

- lifetime employment,
- promotion based on seniority, and
- multiple organizations within the company union,

are signs of such Japanese family-style management. It is not an exaggeration to say that such practices — all of which are weakening currently — support and promote family-style management, which also includes paternalism in the positive sense.

Japanese family-style management does not attempt to distinguish among individuals working in the head office, production plant, and the marketplace or sales department. It is not a discriminatory system. For example, it is not a strict apprentice system that defines and sets standards within a given area, such as in Germany where lines are drawn among corporate managers, plant managers, and supervisors and their workers.

Of course, since the Meiji period, the lamentable custom of putting government above people has become widespread in Japanese society. Even in private corporations, there is a tendency to overemphasize academic credentials and the number of college graduates from the national universities seems to have increased. Yet still, compared to the German system, the wall is not unscalable. The combination of Japanese-style management with the workplace orientation of the well-educated elite created a humane atmosphere within the various workplaces in the corporate structure.

Japan's workplace management was the driving force behind its postwar economy. Workplace management enhanced the quality of the production plant, representative of the workplace. If we were to pinpoint the impetus behind the high level of economic growth from the late 1960s to the late 1970s, it would be workplace management. It was total quality control (TQC) and zero defects (ZD), as well as the Toyota production system. It was managers being committed to the workplace and sending capable personnel into the plants to encourage worker training.

Consequently, the competitive power of Japanese exports increased. We have reached the point now where severe economic friction has surfaced between Japan and the United States, as well as between Japan and Western Europe. Analyzing this strength, namely workplace management, in detail, it is possible to say that Japanese management's strong commitment to the production workplace enabled QC circle activities to develop into TQC management, giving their products an international competitive edge.

However, in this age it is clear that with workplace management focusing on the production plant alone, market needs cannot be grasped whether they be goods or services. Therefore, to attain concrete results, workplace management must be in the forefront of the marketplace surrounded by consumers with their different preferences.

The Toyota production system originally arose as workplace management transcended the production workplace and extended into areas such as the marketplace. This makes it not simply a production system, but a unique Japanese economic system. In fact, "action management" in the form of workplace management will only succeed with a corporate structure always on the lookout for sources of information.

▸ The rise of workplace management in America

"Doing the obvious as the obvious" refers to the realization of principles and theories. However, implementing this doctrine is a difficult task. Importing QC from the United States and transforming it into TQC strengthened the competitive power of Japanese management. Indeed, TQC implementation is "doing the obvious as the obvious." The Toyota production system demands strict implementation of such principles.

For present-day corporations, the marketplace composed of many consumers with divergent values is the information source. With this as a reference point, we must strive to provide the needed amounts of needed goods when they are needed. This must be management's top priority when planning for the twenty-first century. By the way, even American corporations, which at one time eagerly turned to Japan to learn Japanese-style management and implement Japanese TQC, seem to have grasped the essence of things — they are actively advocating and implementing workplace management.

A Passion for Excellence by Tom Peters and Nancy Austin, the sequel to *In Search of Excellence*, states that "true" management involves implementation of the obvious. Furthermore, it explains how difficult attaining this goal might be. Moreover, it advocates "Managing by Wandering Around" (MBWA) as the technology for implementing the obvious. Mr. Peters emphasizes the fact that it is extremely stimulating to wander around the marketplace with the customer to figure out exactly what needs to be done.

No matter how high-powered the computer hardware, it is worthless unless the user can understand the software. For top management to understand customer needs, it is important that managers willingly travel to the marketplace and diligently listen to consumer voices. The authors repeatedly advocate the need to "do the obvious as the obvious," saying that improvements, reformation, as well as innovation are generated by listening to consumers in the marketplace and actually "feeling" the products with them.

Furthermore, the book points out that a distinctive feature of Japanese management is the fact that the subcontractor is a client. The authors explain that Japanese-style management differs from American-style management in the long-term familial relationship between subcontractors and the manufacturer. This is being done today in many successful corporations.

Rather than being subcontractors, these cooperating companies participate as partners bound by the same fate. Not only do they share market information, they themselves serve as information sources, returning information to the manufacturers, namely, their parent companies and their product suppliers. Indeed, this is a distinctive characteristic and a strength of Japanese-style management. However, in this mature economy and evolving information society, present-day corporations require workplace management to incorporate both the overall picture — from multiple perspectives — as well as intricate details.

It is clear that top management, which controls leadership, must be committed to workplace management. However, technological innovation is only possible when the forefront of the marketplace (business and sales departments) unites with both the production workplace (the plant) and research and development, the so-called origin of innovation. Workplace management does not aim simply for cost reduction through vigorous use of production management techniques. The ultimate goal must be the attainment of innovation through the aggressive development of new products and new techniques.

▸ Workplace management: establishing standards

Talking about it is easy — but it is actually difficult to "wander" effectively around the workplace. A manager wandering aimlessly can only bring about more negative results than positive ones. This disturbs people in the workplace and interferes with the work flow.

For the manager wandering around the workplace, signs, charts, data, and standards that accurately measure current workplace conditions are indispensable. Although it is important to converse with the people working in the workplace, visual indicators are more desirable.

It is difficult to establish standards that clearly indicate factors such as the customer preferences and popular phenomena that may foresee future trends. Nonetheless, through close customer contact, we can obtain raw data not available from statistical data. Workplace standards with an ear in the marketplace must be trial and error. Establishing standards this way is one asset of "managing by wandering around."

To see how these standards are set, let's take an example from Toyota — visual standardized operations. During World War II, this was the most essential activity in the Toyota production plant. Skilled mechanics were being sent to the battlefields, one after another, leaving behind male and female workers who were unfamiliar with the machines. This made standard operations even more indispensable. It is not an exaggeration to say that this was the birth of the Toyota production system's workplace management.

As for the process of designing the Toyota production system, we paid attention to the checking of equipment details, positioning of machines, improvement of processing methods, automation innovations, improvement of tools, reevaluation of conveyance operations, rationalization of unfinished work and inventory, and the total elimination of wastes.

We invented *baka-yoke* devices that automatically removed defects, operation errors, and dangerous conditions that could cause accidents. Furthermore, we tried to prevent the recurrence of defects by compiling human information. By doing so, we were able to maintain highly efficient production under human leadership. Standard operations were, after all, the key to success.

A requirement of standard operations is the consideration of various conditions for the pursuit of efficient production, namely, discovering the most effective combination of these factors: human activity, equipment activity, and the product being manufactured. We call this process "combining operations," while "standard operations" refers to the results of these combinations.

The hidden strength of standard operations is that they are unconditionally simplified and utilize visual maintenance standards. The three requisites are:

- Cycle time
- Operations sequence
- Standard inventory

Let's provide each with a simple explanation. "Cycle time," or tact, refers to the time it should take to manufacture a single item. This is determined by the production quantity, in addition to the required number (namely the number of products needed in a given hour according to market demands) and the operating time. The required number can be calculated by dividing the monthly required number by the number of working days. Cycle time can be calculated by dividing the operating time by the daily required number.

Even if cycle time is determined in this manner, individual differences appear among workers. Most of these differences, rather than being ability-oriented, result from differing movements and sequences in the work process. Therefore, certain standards for operations sequences must be established.

Yet before this can happen, the supervisors and managers in the production workplace must exert leadership. Personality and intelligence, as well as a supervisor's enthusiasm and effort, naturally create and cement trust between supervisors and workers, as well as mutual trust between workers. Only with trust, cooperation between sequential processes, and teamwork on a broad level can we attain the three requisites of standardized operations.

"Operations sequence," as expected from the phrase itself, refers to the sequence of operations in the flow of time when a worker is processing a product — such as conveyance, machining, and dismantling. Please note that this does not refer to the assembly-line process.

"Standard inventory" refers to the quantity of unfinished work in process necessary for carrying out operations. Strictly speaking, this number should include products being machined. Within the same machine station, when operations are conducted in the actual manufacturing sequence, only the products being machined are indispensable. In-process inventory is unnecessary. However, if operations ran in the opposite sequence, we would need one item of inventory — two items if two are being machined — between each process.

Since the Toyota production system relies on the just-in-time arrival of parts, standard inventory levels must be firmly established. It is inevitable that if standard inventory is not constantly checked, unnecessary inventory will pile up and defective products will become a major problem.

On a broader level, a company must develop its own standards by creating its own unique management system. Standards must not be imposed by the government or anyone else. It can be said that the Toyota production system itself, based upon Toyota's own philosophy and strategies, is Toyota's management standard. In this sense, the Ford system is also an individually designed standard of large management. Henry Ford warned that uniform standards — not to mention governmental and national standards — must not be imposed on the internal structure of organizations because of their tendency to stifle corporate and individual creativity.

In Henry Ford's time, these problems already existed. Today we are swamped by national standards and increasing numbers of lobbyists. Even Japan Industrial Standards (JIS), which contributed to the rehabilitation of Japan's postwar economy, has finished its task. In this era of sophisticated state-of-the-art technology, standards have become obstacles to corporate and individual creativity. Unless companies establish their own standards, the government and other groups will become even more uncontrollably involved.

Workplace management must be based on establishing unique management standards within individual companies, with managers stationed in the various workplaces.

▸ The search for an all-weather management system usable by anyone

From the very beginning, the Toyota production system dealt with more than the production plant. Considering that market needs come first, namely that all production begins with information (orders) received from the marketplace, the Toyota system is not merely a production system. It was already equipped with the features and essence of a management system.

With the 1973 oil crisis, the Toyota production system became firmly established at Toyota. In the late 1970s, it gradually began spreading beyond Toyota-affiliated companies to other automobile manufacturers and even other industries. Its overall image became one of the model Japanese management systems.

It is true that the Toyota production system originated in Toyota's production plant. Once we grasped how to produce needed goods in the needed quantities at the needed time, reversing our thinking about the production plant, the production system evolved into a management system. This model began with market information and then moved into the production plant to engulf areas of research and development, wherein supposedly lies innovation.

We could say that Japan's economy from the late 1970s to the early 1980s, compared to the haphazard, high-level economic growth of the late 1960s and early 1970s, was a mature economy with a need to balance itself by mastering the use of the accelerator and brakes. However, compared to the stagnating Western European nations and the United States, Japan's economy remains prosperous — and the economic friction between West and East is proceeding from overheated to explosive.

It is clear that under the mature economy the Toyota production system has enjoyed the benefits of economic growth, namely increased demand, and has exerted its strength to reduce costs in the production workplace. In the process, Toyota, as the Toyota management system, has completely eliminated all kinds of waste inside and outside the organization. At the same time, it has firmly established itself as an "all-weather management system":

- keenly attuned to fine changes in the market,
- planning concentrated attacks at the right times,
- devising persistent, wave-like attacks,
- waiting for intermittent chances, and
- minimizing the effects of any unexpected attacks.

Under the mature economy, Toyota mastered the just-in-time management system to deliver needed goods in the needed quantities at the needed time. In this way, it dealt directly with vital market information, or customer orders, and marked the beginning of the Information Age. Companies everywhere appeared to strive for a just-in-time management system.

The JIT management system created by Toyota was generated by turning decision-making around 180 degrees, from the production plant to the marketplace. We have entered an era in which, to survive, retail/service businesses such as large-scale supermarket, restaurant, and convenience store chains, as well as various fast-food companies, must stand in the marketplace armed with the JIT management system.

JIT, which was created by Toyota for secondary industries and originated in the production plant, eventually included the marketplace. On the other hand, the 7-Eleven-style JIT originated in the marketplace for tertiary industries. It is thought that these two JITs eventually will merge to form a completely new management system suitable for the coming sophisticated Information Age.

▸ The limitations of production techniques and the immortality of management systems

We have discussed the fact that the Toyota production system is not simply a collection of production techniques, but a concrete management system. As for the necessity to create such a system, it is clear that outside conditions alone, such as the arrival of the Information Age and the development of a sophisticated information society, fail to explain the situation properly. This is because internal conditions are just as important.

An internal problem, both for the Toyota production system and for TQC, Japanese management's so-called weapon, is how long these production techniques can continue to serve as strengths and assets in managing the production plant. Production techniques can make the most of their strengths only under conditions of high-level economic growth. A pressing issue is the possibility that under a mature economy, when growth begins to taper off, the effectiveness of such production techniques may fade.

An important question is, "Are production techniques themselves the most important tools for management?" Alone their power cannot be exerted fully. Therefore, it is crucial to expand production techniques into a management system.

Even in international economic history, we discover that after England's industrial revolution towards the end of the eighteenth century, its superior economic power, represented by production techniques, was maintained for a long time. However, with the arrival of the twentieth century, American production techniques, represented by the Ford system, toppled England's supremacy and introduced the American Century. By the end of the twentieth century, production techniques represented by TQC and the Toyota production system will surpass those of the United States.

To describe economic history from the eighteenth to the twenty-first century in terms of production techniques and leadership shifts from England to the United States to Japan is too simplistic. The source of wealth for emerging industrial nations always lies in production — and production techniques alone support and promote production. It is even more interesting to consider why supremacy in production techniques — the economic driving force — moved from England to the United States to Japan. Does the power of production techniques naturally weaken when economic growth stagnates and production levels off? Does this mean that while hardware is effective, software is useless? Or is it because they remained at the production-techniques level, unable to intertwine these techniques into the larger framework of the management system?

Japan presently stands at the crossroads between an industrial and an information society, facing ordeals it has never experienced before.

▾

Dialogue: Place of imagination, place of convergence, place of decision

Mito: The term "workplace management" first conjures up active images. In journalism, workplace management refers to flying to the scene of an event, imprinting it in our minds, and reliving the event immediately before doing anything else. If we say we can think before or during running or walking, then a journalist's workplace management can be described as rushing to the scene before thinking about it. However, even in this case, there are various locations besides that of this primary scene.

It goes without saying that the scene of an event is a journalist's major workplace. However, investigating background information pertaining to the occurrence, searching for and interviewing individuals directly and indirectly involved — all of these involve different locations, or workplaces. In other words, journalists naturally drift toward places and people in which new and rare information can be found. Any location serving as such an information source can be labeled "a workplace."

Since your workplace management incorporates every workplace in the Toyota production system, from conception to final assembly, it is extremely valuable. Mr. Ohno, where is your workplace?

Ohno: I would say it is the production plant. I entered Toyoda Spinning and Weaving in 1932. Since it has been over half a century since I was transferred to Toyota Motors' production plant, any other workplace would seem insignificant to me. The production plant is so stimulating. The more involved you become, the more problems emerge — and you never want to leave.

Through confrontations as well as through harmony between machines and workers, quality products are created. Even a little carelessness, however, will produce waste rapidly in the form of defects. Therefore, the production plant is at once a free and generous creature and an insidious and mischievous nuisance. Those who work there are fascinated by the challenge of discovering ways to deal with this entity.

Harmony and discord aside, a vital production plant cannot operate unless people assume leadership and bring out the best of the machines and the system. To do so, people must utilize their intelligence and imagination to improve their work environment as well as investigate problems in the production plant. Production people should experience all different environments such as visiting car dealerships. We all have a principle workplace — but don't most of us also have several sub-workplaces perhaps not apparent to others? To generate new information and trigger the imagination, a critical mind needs different environments.

We can consider mental workplaces in terms of imagination, conveyance (for organizing thoughts), and decisionmaking. The imagination workplace of the venerable Toyoda Sakichi was inspiring and overwhelming. Toyoda Kiichirō's innovation, imagination, and foresight in the production plant were immeasurable yet practical, providing us with dreams and hope. Each of these pioneers developed a distinctive imaginative workplace from which we still have much to learn.

▸ Kobayashi Ichizo's workplace management of the future

Mito: The workplace management of Kobayashi Ichizo is extremely interesting. On one hand, he was a novelist, a screenwriter, the founder of Osaka's Hankyu Group, and the organizer of the Toei movie theater and Takarazuka Theater Group. On the other hand, he revived Nihon Keikinzoku (Japan Light Metals) and rebuilt Tokyo Dento (Tokyo Electric Light, the present Tokyo Denki's predecessor). Before World War II, he was Minister of Commerce and Industry and withdrew from the elections for Prime Minister. A person of varied accomplishments, he has continued to exert his entrepreneurial spirit.

For example, in both the case of the Imperial Theater and the Takarazuka Theater Group, Mr. Kobayashi used various strategies to identify what the general public would call true entertainment. In such circumstances, Mr. Kobayashi had various workplaces to stimulate his imagination. For a long time, and especially since he began commercializing mass entertainment, he frequented Tokyo's Asakusa district because it offered genuine popular entertainment. Here — where the Jazz Age was introduced in Japan — he developed a real feeling for the masses. This practice was somewhat intimidating.

He saw Asakusa as the seedbed of mass entertainment. Ginza, Tokyo's Western-style shopping district, and Shinjuku, the city's night life center, he felt, were nothing but stores. His curiosity was not aroused by "new" things — but by the rare or unusual. He would wonder how they came about there. He declared that those who really stimulated public sentiment, such as comedians Furukawa Roppa and Enoki Kenichi, and actor Kikuta Kazuo, were spawned in the Asakusa district. There they became accomplished entertainers, later appearing in the large theaters.

Mr. Kobayashi's workplace management involves walking around to see for himself the type of entertainment atmosphere being generated and the types of performances being given by successful entertainers. This can be a difficult task requiring a firm commitment to knowledge from everyday art, culture, the performing arts, and the artists themselves. In today's age, when the "segmented public" (*bunshu*) is no longer the "general public" (*taishu*), it will take immense curiosity to surpass Mr. Kobayashi's workplace management.

Ohno: It took insight to pinpoint the Asakusa district and recognize that new arts come from the masses. All businesses have a "store" as well as a seedbed of creativity that must be dealt with accordingly. Only a critical, curious mind with a wide range of activities could recognize this.

▸ Honda Soichiro's workplace management and action-orientation

Mito: Besides the production plant, wasn't the American supermarket — even though you had never seen one — your imagination workplace?

Ohno: We talk about workplace management and action-orientation, but both Toyoda Sakichi and Toyoda Kiichirō worked in the factory with a purpose. Ideas crossed their minds constantly. Saying that isolating themselves in their offices did not solve problems, they would walk over to the production plant.

There were also times when, on the verge of a new idea, they would decide to take a walk around the plant. Often they would be struck by an idea when coming across a certain scene in the production plant. Newton saw the apple fall and observed a clue to the law of gravity. Physicist Yukawa Hideki (1907–1981) came up with the meson theory suddenly while in bed. Such occurrences happen only by thinking things over again and again.

A model of workplace management and action-orientation is the story of Toyoda Sakichi, in his earnest pursuit of an automatic loom, standing and watching a neighbor woman operating a hand loom. After a period of observation, he began to understand clearly the rhythm of the loom as well as its mechanism. More and more fabric was woven and he found himself fascinated. What formidable concentration and imagination! This is what happens when thinking exceeds all boundaries — it explodes.

We could call Toyoda Kiichirō's devotion to vehicles for domestic use also a mental explosion. Although a different type, Honda Soichiro's workplace management and action-orientation are filled fundamentally with the desire to accomplish things at any cost.

Mito: Indeed, Mr. Honda personifies workplace management and action-orientation. Prior to World War II, he came into direct contact with European and American cars and became familiar with the amazing power and capacity of their engines. Therefore, after the war, he started from scratch and refused to become a Toyota subcontractor, instead choosing independence. He already knew what engine standards should be should he ever decide to get into the motorcycle or automobile business.

Mr. Honda needed to feel the power of an engine by grasping the steering wheel. He once remodeled a Ford car and entered a race. He was in an accident at the finish line and narrowly escaped death. Rather than dampening his interest in engines, however, the incident inspired him. "People don't die easily. It was a good experience for me," he said, and became even more obsessed by engines. During the war, he was restrained by the government and military, unable to do the work he loved. We can understand why he mentally "exploded" at the war's end in 1945.

Ohno: It is evident that Mr. Honda was familiar with technical standards for U.S. and Western European motorcycles and automobiles prior to the war. After all, Japan didn't produce any vehicles resembling cars. The only ones available were imported from General Motors and Ford.

From early on, Mr. Honda studied foreign cars in detail. After starting his own business after the war, he had one clear objective — namely, to create an engine equal to and capable of surpassing those of the United States and Western Europe. This furious drive is the essence of workplace management and action-orientation.

Mito: In the beginning of 1960, I interviewed Mr. Honda. I still remember how surprised I was when he emerged from a shabby building that was full of smoke and the noise of engines. While outgoing and cheerful, he was obviously obsessed by something.

In his fifties at the time, he was running tests to increase drastically the number of engine revolutions in an attempt to create his own efficient, high-powered engine. I sensed a kind of insanity, the presence of some type of spirit. Perhaps the term "insanity" is inappropriate. However, for Mr. Honda, as well as for both Toyoda men, perhaps it is this type of insanity that assumes control when struggling to attain a goal.

Perhaps, Mr. Ohno, you, too, were once in the same situation.

▸ Revealing the subliminal

Ohno: Whether we can call it insanity or not, when obsessed by our work, we often come up with unexpected and astonishing ideas. This is probably because insanity stimulates imagination. If we were to describe what happens when we go crazy, we might call it a fascination with thinking, or an immeasurable passion to pursue and solve problems. It is a problem-solving monologue. One question emerges after another. *Why? Why? Why?* These *why's* begin to converge in the direction of an explanation for the true essence of the problem.

Originally, the goal of the Toyota production system was to eliminate waste, waste being particularly common in the production area. Once we started eliminating waste, we decided to go ahead and eliminate it completely. Since waste is infinite, we will never be satisfied. Therefore, we will continue creatively to destroy the Toyota production system. It is my feeling that when layers of *why's* accumulate in our minds, our nerves are strained to the point of insanity.

From the late 1950s until the late 1960s, when anything produced could be sold, the "big guns and warships" orientation predominated. Anyone could see that sales profits would increase markedly if more goods were produced and sold. At the same time, every supervisor in the production plant knew that waste, too, would be mass-produced.

But corporations that emphasized increased production felt that increased sales, rather than innovative methods to eliminate waste, reflected success. This was the trap. Wastes are direct obstacles to profit. No matter how high the sales, valuable profits can dissipate in the form of waste.

I remember, in the process of constructing the Toyota production system, images of profits scattering this way, while empty containers accumulated through sales. Although just an imaginary situation, insanity was responsible for it. For both large and small problems, if we repeat *why* five times to solve it, we are safe. If we are obsessed by a determination to do things, whether right or wrong, some outside shock eventually will trigger an explosion. Perhaps this is "revealing the subliminal."

▸ Repeating *why* five times and proving our hypothesis

Mito: Of course, it is not easy to repeat *why* five times in order to prove our hypothesis. Let's analyze the Toyota production system.

First, there is "Toyota-style production," or how to run operations, which shapes the production flow, or work flow. On top of Toyota-style production comes the *kanban* system with its two types of information, "withdrawal kanban" and "production kanban," an operations technique that maintains just-in-time production. Kanban provides the needed goods in the needed amounts at the needed time. Of course, it is essentially the combination of the five *why's* that enables us to proceed this far. However, to bury the old "big guns and warships" mentality, answering any one of these five *why's* is a difficult task.

For instance, such a mentality might be able to increase sales. Yet just as there are mountains, there are also valleys. With excessive waste, profits scatter like water in a sieve.

Therefore, by demolishing the mountain, we bury the valleys. An economic disposition not subject to the whims of the marketplace seems indispensable. Let's say our hypothesis, or presumption, is to shift to standardized production. Of course, it is not easy to ask *why* persistently. However, once prospects become visible, the workers in the production plant probably will propose various steps for reform.

Ohno: To create the production flow and establish an overall structure for just-in-time production, we visited car dealerships and deepened our understanding of *pulling* goods from the production plant in the needed amounts at the needed time. As a model, the supermarket was perfect for building an overall image of just-in-time production. At this stage, we could conjure up concrete strategies for standardized production but the problem was how to make decisions.

The main difference between the "big guns and warships"-oriented Ford system and the standardized production-style Toyota system is the setup process for the die presses.

For years, the Ford system has used the quantity of sheet metal produced in a given time period as an indicator of productivity. In other words, it has adopted maximum lot sizes and minimum setup and adjustment procedures as its primary objective.

In contrast, the Toyota system's standardized production strives to keep mountains as small as possible. Furthermore, it attempts to reduce lot sizes gradually in order to eventually produce each and every product uniquely. This small-lot orientation reflects the foresight of this generation and conformity to the diversity of values in the Information Age. Moreover, it is similar to convenience stores, the so-called information stores currently existing in the marketplace.

We have wandered from the topic of insanity to that of the five *why's*. Basically, if you can repeat *why* five times, things will gradually become interesting. Proving hypotheses is fascinating. Furthermore, we should appreciate the fact that we can obtain valuable hints from the production plant. Of course, in many cases, you alone are the only one who finds such things interesting. Perhaps this is wherein lies insanity.

▸ That which stimulates imagination: insanity

Mito: A while ago, you referred to the fact that, repressed feelings can surface when triggered by an outside stimulus. Isn't it abnormal for one to be so obsessed by a pressing problem that one represses it? Perhaps that is where the insanity is.

Inamori Kazuo, current chairman of Kyocera Corporation, the entrepreneur of new materials like "fine ceramic" and the developer of the Crescent Vert line of synthetic gemstones, in his overwhelming enthusiasm toward the information industry, often remarks that no technological development is unsolvable if one's desire is so passionate and pure that it sinks into the subliminal. He also admits that this process of thinking about something until it descends into the subliminal is insanity.

Certainly, in your case, as well as in the cases of Honda Soichiro and Mr. Inamori, it can be said that this type of insanity was what enabled you to develop and construct new products, techniques, and systems. The term "insanity" possesses negative connotations in Western culture. It implies deviation from normality. However, in the Far East, including Japan, insanity is often seen as part of normality, as in the saying "genius is just one step from insanity."

Here we have the pair of words "genius" and "lunatic." I think the term "genius" can be applied to all the arts. Yet even so, anticipating counterarguments such as "what do lunatics have to do with entrepreneurs and managers?" and "how are entrepreneurs, managers, and madmen related?" I would like to explain further. Frankly, I think of entrepreneurs and managers as leaders of organizations and artists of organizational management. They never make decisions under the same circumstances or patterns but are always involved in creative work. Of course, the type differs, but artists do not have a monopoly on insanity. By reexamining artistic imagination and insanity, we can come up with a lot of ideas.

Involved in state-of-the-art work in the fields of psychiatry and psychopathology, Professor Iwai Kan, Department of Psychiatry, St. Marianne Medical School, in his book *Insanity as Humanism*, highlights three links between insanity and imagination:

1. Insanity allows us to experience things we normally do not experience, things that transcend the ordinary.
2. Insanity veers away from normality as does genius, but in the opposite direction. On occasion, however, the two merge, and our imagination is stimulated.
3. The bitterness of insanity often leads to a strengthening of spirit that sometimes influences imagination.

I am not saying that insanity itself is the ability to imagine. However, it is reasonable to say that insanity stimulates and enhances imagination in some way or another.

Ohno: It is often said that while pursuing our goal with manic devotion in the production plant or research lab, we begin to lose zeal because the surroundings become too comfortable or familiar. This is untrue.

Organizational leaders must comprehend factors such as inner and outer environmental changes and the demands and directions of the times. Based on these factors, the corporation must indicate what must be done from the top-down. In the production plant, from the bottom-up, employees must propose ways to improve human relations, increase productivity, and ultimately reduce costs through improvements to their own workplaces.

I believe it is this harmony and discord, the magnified effect between the top-down and bottom-up styles, that causes insanity in the minds of people working there.

Based on my experiences in the production plant, I know that in the beginning, people tended to resist change, whether large or small, making the atmosphere unconducive to implementing change. However, if the employees were frantic, we were crazy! In the end, we forced our way through and persuaded the others. The whole process of developing the Toyota production system took place this way. From the late 1940s to the early 1960s, with everyone in opposition, it was called the "abominable Ohno production system." People refused to call it the "Toyota production system." When I confirmed the validity of the system and tried to implement it, everyone objected vehemently. To overcome this resistance, I had to quarrel and fight. And since the numbers were against me, I had no choice — I went crazy. This differs from an "ambitious spirit."

▸ Establishing our own standards: a supreme order

Mito: Speaking of workplace management, "Managing By Wandering Around" (MBWA) has become extremely popular among American managers. Tom Peters states that since American managers rarely travel to both the marketplace and the production plant, they cannot grasp the needs of consumers nor understand how to manufacture good, defect-free products. Therefore, he advocates MBWA. While Mr. Peters seems overly sensitive to Japanese corporations, workplace management is an indispensable condition for managers. However, if managers simply make an appearance without a set purpose, MBWA is harmless — and also profitless.

Mr. Ohno, as the inventor/developer of the Toyota production system and someone who still goes to the production plant whenever you can, what do you consider workplace management's objective?

Ohno: I mentioned this before, but the objective of MBWA is to establish our own checkpoints. To grasp the public's needs by standing in the marketplace, we need superior insight and imagination, like that of Kobayashi Ichizo. To be able to compare the Asakusa, Ginza, and Shinjuku districts of Tokyo and make value judgments on their characters and essence, measurements and standards are indispensable.

This is also true of the production plant where the most basic standard, as I often say, has to be to handwrite the standardized operations. These standards must be posted in each production area so that everyone can see at a glance (1) what type of workplace it is, (2) what the production amount is, and (3) what the sequence of operations should be. This is fundamental and the model for *visual control*. If such standards are posted around the production plant, MBWA effectiveness will increase dramatically. The group, applying such standards from top to bottom, will become extremely responsive and develop a level of common awareness towards work. Furthermore, with these standards as a base, it is generally easier for entrepreneurs and managers to present standards from the top-down. Employees in the production plant, too, will make more precise bottom-up proposals.

Looking back to when we were developing and applying the Toyota production system, our main concern was *to do the obvious as the obvious*. Naturally, leaders must not copy other companies but ultimately must develop organizational models and systems suited to their situations.

At Toyota, we first established Toyota-style production, which regulated production flow. We then continued to work on the just-in-time system for providing us with needed goods in the needed amounts at the needed time. Then we created the kanban system, as a means of implementing the just-in-time system and communicating information. During this process, it was the contrasting Ford system that stimulated our spirit.

Because we talked figuratively about destroying Ford's so-called absolute standard, which had spread all over the world, some people probably thought of us as fearless "Don Quixotes." If the Ford system was an extraordinary standard, then I think the Toyota production system will become equally remarkable.

▸ Don't rely excessively on governmental standards!

Mito: Since corporations must survive under free competition with self-responsibility, they must establish management standards to suit their needs. Mr. Ohno's idea that the Toyota production system is Toyota's own standard is quite unique.

Henry Ford certainly emphasizes this point also, but each corporation must develop its own standards. Standards should not be imposed by the government. While governmental standards, such as the Japan Industrial Standards (JIS), played a crucial role in postwar recovery and return to the international economic arena, excessive reliance on such standards blocks progress. In this age of sophisticated, state-of-the-art technology, JIS functions as a cartel-like conservative, becoming an obstacle to the imagination of corporations. We need creative destruction.

A long time ago, Henry Ford warned us that although governmental standards might be good temporarily, eventually management's goal would be to maintain such standards and corporations would forget about consumer needs.

Ohno: Basics such as weight and measure should be standardized on an international level. However, corporate standards should reflect strongly the imagination and characteristics of individual workplaces. Otherwise, they will not be fully assimilated.

Posting standards in production areas taps the creativity and innovation of any workplace. The result is the formation of unexpected cooperative relationships and increased production efficiency. No matter how advanced the automated equipment or robots become, human beings still will control them. The resulting standards will be human. This is what we should treasure.

As seen in the Toyota production system, TQC, and ZD, the efforts to improve quality and eliminate defects depend on individual creativity, innovation, mutual cooperation, and teamwork.

▸ Individual corporate culture came first

Mito: Both TQC and ZD, which Japanese corporations are implementing tirelessly, were originally manufacturing techniques used in American production plants. Adopting them after the war, Japan progressed significantly through development of its own QC circle, or small group, activities. Through the late 1950s, 1960s, and 1970s, quality control infiltrated the corporations and circle activities were implemented companywide. Gradually, QC has come to be applied not only to products, but to management as well.

Once in Japan, American-style QC became part of Japan's own TQC — "total quality control with total employee involvement" or "total quality control through overall inspection of management." Now recognized throughout the world as one of Japanese management's most powerful weapons, managers and technicians from all over the world come to Japan to study it. Furthermore, it is being exported to many countries as Japan invests capital in building factories abroad.

TQC management occurs in the following way. The explicit intentions of upper management permeate the whole organization through a top-down mechanism. At the same time, innovative ideas of employees are absorbed by small group activities through a bottom-up mechanism. Both parties stimulate each other and the process repeats itself over and over. The longer this continues, the closer we come to the essence of TQC.

By the way, if everyone starts to use TQC, we certainly will find examples of failure. Looking at those failures, I feel many people think TQC is management's sole purpose, even though it was originally designed as a management technique or tool. If we then ask what should be management's purpose, I would answer, "critical awareness of individual corporations," or "individual corporate culture." Let me elaborate.

Take Toyota, for example. Before TQC, to eliminate wastes totally, we had to plan and work towards implementing the Toyota production system. We seriously tackled TQC implementation in the early 1960s, winning the Deming Award in 1965 and the coveted Japan Quality Control Award in 1970.

Long before its implementation, Toyota- or Ohno-style manufacturing techniques had been put steadily through grueling tests. By the time TQC was implemented, these techniques had been promoted to being called the Toyota production system. TQC helped disseminate and stabilize the system.

To utilize TQC as a management technique, corporations must attain their own management goals, as we did with the construction of the Toyota production system. Otherwise, efforts will be in vain.

Ohno: Aren't TQC and ZD both concrete methods of attaining management objectives? Likewise, aren't there times when QC circle activities slowly help clarify management objectives by asking about corporate goals and the role of the manager? From corporate managers who have thoroughly researched and successfully implemented TQC, I have heard that, while it is an effective management technique, TQC can be developed into a management philosophy or even a management objective. These views are probably justifiable.

I wholly approve of improving the overall — as opposed to "partial" — quality of management by increasing the sphere of small-group activities, as in the case of TQC and ZD. I also strongly support the zero-defects movement, which strives to eliminate defects from various work areas. As an entity, the Toyota production system clearly exists on a different level from TQC and ZD.

Mito: From the time the Toyota production system was the Ohno system, you strived to improve Toyota's manufacturing techniques and all production workplaces. This shows your clear sense of purpose. Even as other methods of promoting and attaining these goals materialized, it is clear that your system sustained such efforts. However, I want to emphasize again the fact that the Toyota production system served as both a management goal and as a means of supporting the goal.

It goes without saying that for the success of the Toyota production system, as well as TQC and ZD, the company president, namely the leader of the corporate structure, must shoulder all responsibility and exert leadership.

▸ The president is responsible for 100 percent — not 85 percent

Mito: W. Edwards Deming, for whom the Deming Prize was named, after praising Japan's TQC, declared that 85 percent of the responsibility to make TQC succeed lies with the president who controls the leadership. As long as TQC is supposed to be company-wide, it is the president's responsibility to put his or her own authority to the test. In reality, few cases fail for this reason. They fail because of imitation.

With the 1973 oil crisis, the Toyota production system infiltrated the entire Toyota group and its affiliated companies. In the late 1970s, it transcended the Toyota consortium as well as the industry. Indeed, the Toyota production system seems to be no longer "Toyota-style" but "Japan-style". It also seems to have advanced to a higher dimension, evolving from a simple production system to a management system.

The goals and matters being pursued by the members of the New Production System (NPS) Research Association, to which you also belong, are clearly based on the Toyota production system. Furthermore, they are surpassing it. To master TQC, ZD, the Toyota production system, and NPS, the president must exert unwavering leadership and be committed to realizing such goals at all costs.

Ohno: I'm not sure where the 85 percent of Professor Deming's presidential responsibility comes from, but traditional American management customarily compiles instructional manuals on all management techniques and works according to what has been written. In most cases, a serious lack of humane leadership in the area of workplace management on the part of the president probably existed. Therefore, even 50 percent seems like an overestimation. For American management in the past, 85 percent indicates an inconceivable sense of responsibility.

I think the Toyota production system's success depends on the president assuming 100-percent responsibility. To implement it, we must involve the corporation and all affiliated corporations. At this point, the system is no longer just a production system, but a management system that promotes management innovation in all participating companies on all levels.

The Toyota production system has transcended the Toyota group and spread to various industries. Despite its widespread dissemination, it will not succeed without a strong critical awareness. It should always be inquiring: "What are the corporation's objectives?" "What is the best atmosphere for the corporation?" and "What type of corporate culture should be encouraged?" Under these circumstances, mere imitation will not work.

Even if one actually implements the Toyota production system, it makes little sense to do so unless it is ultimately embraced as the *X* production system or, more accurately, the *X* management system, crowned with the name of the corporation. For this to happen, the president must realize that he or she is completely responsible.

The members of the NPS Research Association are a new corporate group that, through the development of the Toyota production system, is zealously pursuing a production or management system for the new age. In NPS, everything is practiced with the critical awareness that the president has total responsibility. Composed of one company from each industry, this multi-industry group is immersed day and night in the creative construction of a *new production system*. Inevitably, the results of their common goal will surpass our imagination. Since member presidents issue commands to bear 100 percent of the responsibility, visible positive results will emerge.

Members have different histories and dissimilar backgrounds. Some have been financially on the brink. However, the strength of the current NPS members lies in the fact that they practice management by always asking themselves, "What are our corporate goals?" and imposing the most stringent conditions on themselves. Most corporations would not assume such a management posture unless faced by war or some adversity.

Mito: It is not only managers who fail to have a true sense of impending crisis until they are actually driven into misfortune. This is "human weakness" in both the East and West.

Peter F. Drucker, who gained access to many corporations as a management consultant thinking with and advising managers, points this out. Usually, only when a company falls on bad times does upper management ask "What *is* our business?" and "What are our goals?" He stresses that we should ask these questions seriously when we are successful. With TQC, ZD, the Toyota production system, and NPS, I think it makes more sense to pursue earnestly a management system that prepares for the worst under favorable rather than adverse circumstances.

▸ How Japanese corporations will perpetuate the superiority of production techniques

Mito: Mr. Ohno, you pointed out the Toyota production system is no longer a simple production system, but that it has already evolved into a management system. As a production system only, it certainly will have its limits. In any case, TQC and the Toyota production system have become known worldwide as Japan's most powerful management weapon and the driving force behind its competitive economic power.

I think these methods are seen mainly as concerns of the production plant and as production techniques. With such limited views, the decline of Japan's economic strength and competitive power cannot be far off. Warnings and constructive criticism are beginning to come from all directions.

One memorable criticism was Professor Kichikawa Hiroyuki's suggestion. He is currently continuing his research in precision machinery engineering in the University of Tokyo's Department of Engineering. In his book *Robots and Humans*, Professor Kichikawa touches upon the essence of production techniques. He identifies those used in advanced countries and states that production techniques are most effective when demand is infinite.

In other words, he warns us that economic growth has its limits, and that Japan, entering a age of mature economy, cannot continue to rely on the superiority of its production techniques. He also remarks that production techniques should be considered as transient. What are your thoughts on this subject?

Ohno: You mentioned this before, but the end of the Toyota production system will be very near if it is limited to being a production technique. However, since it continues to transform itself qualitatively toward becoming a management system, I think it can survive for a long time.

Our industrial structure is shifting from heavy industries to the service — or "soft" — sector, symbolized by the frivolous and insignificant. This is a more serious issue. Take the automobile industry as an example. If we simply were to make cars — or hardware — by mechanically processing raw materials and assembling various parts, sooner or later we would reach a limit to qualitative growth.

Proceeding in this direction, formidable rivals such as Korea surely will emerge, one after another, as threats to Japan. To overcome this, we must somehow fit software into the hardware. The key to survival in the twenty-first century is in creating a new industry that combines these two.

▸ The Toyota production system as a universal management system

Ohno: I seem to be repeating myself, but the Toyota production system is no longer a production system. As long as we aim for a universal management system, perhaps we don't need to worry about what we call it. However, as long as we promote the Toyota production system and its twin pillars of autonomation and just-in-time, I believe the name itself is universal.

The reason I continue to mention the switch from a production to a management system is because it implies *cost-down* for management. Thus, cost-down does not refer to just cost reductions in the production plant, but to overall management checks and the search for and total elimination of waste.

The true essence of the new management system assumes the elimination of waste in the production workplace and the actualization of cost reduction. It must be equipped with a powerful engine that can adapt to the everchanging needs of the market, aggressively raise questions, and promote the research and development of new products and techniques.

Although in its present form the Toyota production system might be difficult to implement in the United States, Europe, and Southeast Asia, we have now entered an era in which portions of it are beginning to be understood on a wider scale. Therefore, it would seem stranger if the Toyota production system itself did not evolve and change.

Mito: When the Toyota production system develops into a management system, what will happen to its name? You said that in the sense that the system's essence was provided by Toyoda Sakichi and Toyoda Kiichirō, the name is universal and will always be the Toyota production system. However, it is up to corporations to modify it and name systems after themselves.

We can interpret this as the beginning of the self-destruction and self-propagation of the Toyota production system, washed by external and internal waves of diverse value. A new management system suited to our sophisticated Information Age will emerge.

▼

Mito's Commentary A

▸ How will the workplace management of Kobayashi Ichizo, developed with the public in mind, fit this new age of middle-class diversity?

Kobayashi Ichizo (1873–1957) was a man of freedom and imagination. He wrote novels, plays, and even musicals. He was a realist, an eminent authority on contemporary sensibility, and at the same time a remarkable romanticist.

A disciple of Fukuzawa Yukichi of Mita, Mr. Kobayashi started out as a banker for Mitsui Bank. Midway, he became disillusioned. The Koshu-born Kobayashi then moved to Kansai, where he started popularizing the service and entertainment businesses. Later, he created the present Hankyu group businesses, including railways, hot spring resorts, theatrical groups, and department stores.

He immersed himself in his businesses, dreaming of the advent of mass consumerism in Japan. He believed that only companies that looked ahead would succeed. Eventually, he returned to Tokyo.

Today, the mass consumer society has passed. Under materially affluent conditions, the public has divided into coexisting segmented, small groups. The industrial world is trying hard to cope with the situation. Tsutsumi Seiji of the Seibu-Saison Group, Nakauchi Ko of Daiei, and Itoh Masatoshi of Ito Yokado as individuals have attempted to interpret the "segmented group" psychology in order to create stores and develop real estate. Does their interpretation of the times transcend that of Mr. Kobayashi's? Mr. Tsutsumi and Mr. Nakauchi have always been aware of his business results. A true indication of having surpassed Mr. Kobayashi would be to become a pioneer in the hitherto unexplored sophisticated information society.

No entrepreneur has surpassed Mr. Kobayashi's mass appeal. To understand the nature of the new segmented groups and to attain concrete results, we must devise innovative schemes that surpass Mr. Kobayashi's workplace management.

Fields and stores are different

Let's look at Kobayashi Ichizo's thoughts on mass appeal. The story is about Tokyo's Asakusa district, but the basic idea can be transferred to any time or place.

> For people to work in good health and with enthusiasm, they must communicate with the masses. In practicing business, I never forget that my work is with the public. Therefore, whenever I have free time, I try to go to the Takarazuka resort or hang out in

Asakusa. Perhaps this is one way my lifestyle differs from that of other people.

As for Asakusa, we often refer to it in the context of "the masses," but these masses epitomize the general public. Unlike other districts of the city, Asakusa does not cater to the upper class. The rich and famous do not parade around Asakusa. In fact, it is not really an area where one can strut. There are gathering places in the Ginza, Shinjuku, and Shibuya districts where the affluent and the intellectuals can be seen.

Where do our standards for judging something as low-class or inferior come from? Asakusa's culture has its own respectable value. Much of the art is unfinished and confused. However, we cannot look down our noses at the immense power and creativity emanating from this chaos. This power cannot be found elsewhere.

I think of Asakusa as a seedbed or field. New things only can be conceived and grown in a field. Ginza and Shinjuku are "stores." There, finished products are simply put on display. When we see something new in a store, we pick it up to look at it. Nothing else happens. On the other hand, when we find something rare in a field, we wonder why it grew there and how to take care of it. We can attempt to possess it. Once we have mastered it, we can sell it all over the country. The reason I am attracted still to Asakusa is because I can observe freely such seedbeds of creativity.

The Imperial Theater recently has taken a new course by sponsoring musicals. This is an incredibly difficult task, made possible by the genius of Hata Toyokichi. However, I think it is premature. These performances are of the type that need to be nurtured slowly in the "fields" of Asakusa, rather than suddenly being dragged in a crude form to the theatrical storefront. Since all occupations and businesses have a "storefront" and a "field," it is important to distinguish between the two and treat them accordingly. If we make the wrong decision and bring out something to the storefront too soon, there will be waste and possible bankruptcy. These considerations are extremely crucial for entrepreneurs. Humility and diligence as well as care and patience are demanded if the "seed" is to become a presentable product.

In other words, all businesses target the masses. Every facet of work is related to the public. Far from holding the masses in contempt, the key to future success lies in our unwavering respect for them as our teacher.

▸ Honda Soichiro's respect for logic, ideas, and time

Honda Soichiro, born in 1906, is still as youthful as an adolescent at the age of 80. The essence of his bold yet scrupulous management is a respect for people. The following principles reflect the Hondaism of Honda Motor's corporate spirit:

- Do not imitate others
- Do not depend on the government
- Work for yourself

Mr. Honda's seemingly reckless behavior was sustained by his scientific respect for logic, ideas, and time. His mind, forced to behave according to his passions, housed a strong respect for human individuality and consideration for others. The spirit of Hondaism instilled by Mr. Honda and his colleague, Fujisawa Takeo, still promotes powerful individuality and personality. In Mr. Honda's case, the spirit is accompanied by an active body. Here are some excerpts from his writings — they are his life principles as well as those Honda Motor is striving to attain.

> I will never forget. It was July, 1936, and I was 31.
>
> The spacious stadium, fortified with concrete, had grass on one side and bleachers on the other. It was filled with spectators. In front of me, a straight, wide racing line had been drawn. At the point where the white line started to blend in with the green of the lawn and the surroundings, a red flag fluttered from left to right.
>
> In my field of vision, I could see seven or eight of the racers intently checking their engines. We were so immersed in our preparations that we hardly could hear the clamor of each other's engines. It seemed like my younger brother, sitting in the assistant driver's seat, felt the same way. Our car was a refurbished Ford. It was not only fast, but designed by us not to flip over on sharp turns.
>
> Praying in my heart, "Come on, you can do it, you've got to win, please win..." I lightly patted the body of my car, the fruit of my labors. It felt like my turtleneck jacket was strangling me so that the blood in my head couldn't circulate. As usual, my legs were shaking.

Eventually, the starter blew the "ready" whistle. For a moment, I felt as if the air around me had froze. Through the glass, crouched in the car, I could see the goal sign far away, flickering on and off, enticing me.

The signal gun fired, and we were off. I opened the throttle as far as it would go. With a thunderous blast, leaving trails of thick smoke, my cherished car shot out like a huge bullet. It seemed as if the roar of the engine was reverberating inside me. Immersed in this feeling, I operated the steering wheel. On the flat racetrack it seemed as if my car was being sucked into a mass of running clouds.

One hundred, 110, and then 120 kilometers per hour... our speed increased rapidly. As expected, we were ahead. As the goal loomed into sight, a car being repaired suddenly entered the track from the side. We collided. In the next moment, my car rolled over two or three times. I had no time to think. In a matter of seconds, I felt my body spinning and my field of vision collapsing. At that moment, we had been going more than 130 kilometers per hour.

Pushed from the car, I was knocked to the ground. From there I bounced and was struck again. I lost consciousness.

When I awoke, I felt so much pain, my face felt like it was being immersed in boiling water. However, under the pain, I realized I was really alive. As I fell back into my state of unconsciousness, I remembered my brother.

"He's fine. It is amazing that both of you are alive."

I could see the face of the nurse, smiling at me. I had smashed the left side of my face, dislocated my shoulder, and broken my wrist. My brother had broken four ribs. We were so lucky and, strangely, I was impressed by the fact that people don't die easily. People scolded me, saying, "You shouldn't be impressed by such things. You're too easygoing."

Thinking back on it, on one hand I feel as if I was too reckless, but on the other hand, I remember it fondly, as if it had been a pleasant event. I recall feeling that my purpose in life was to sacrifice my body and spirit for speed itself. It is definitely true that I shall retain that dream within me.

Furthermore, I would like to mention that our team was awarded the winning trophy on the basis of our astonishing speed prior to the collision.[3]

Factories don't need warehouses!

The story of Honda Soichiro is extremely inspiring. The hair-raising experience in the auto race fueled his obsession just as his challenging spirit generated Honda Motor's corporate spirit.

At this point, I would like to comment on the breadth and depth of Mr. Honda's concept of workplace management and action orientation. Taiichi Ohno, in judgment, declared Mr. Honda not only a genius in engine-making, but also very humane, in his goal of creating an ultra-rational production workplace. We can find evidence for this by rummaging through some of Mr. Honda's older writings. An essay called "What Are Techniques?" published in 1960 exemplifies this:

> Life comes from three types of wisdom: seeing, hearing, and trying. I think that among these three, the most important one is *trying*. Yet most technicians emphasize seeing and hearing and neglect trying. Of course, I, too, see and hear, but try even more. It may seem obvious, but failure and success are opposites. As happiness and sorrow coexist, so do failure and success. We seem to succeed more often than we fail. Everyone detests failure, so there are fewer opportunities to succeed. People seem surprised with Honda's success, but the only secret is that we know what we are doing. My intention is stronger than that of other technicians because I try harder. There is a big difference between reading a book and giving instructions, and attempting something first and then giving instructions. In the latter case, we feel confident. That is why I think trying is the most important factor.[4]

We can also detect hints of ultra-rationalization to rival the Toyota production system. In his essay "Sweat and Imagination," Mr. Honda discusses workerpower and automation, highlighting how wasteful automation and mechanization are. He states that our priority should be to eliminate the mountains of waste surrounding us, not to demand the implementation of newly-invented, large-scale, high-speed equipment. He also proclaims that if we lack the funds, rationalization should be attempted. Moreover, it is possible. This overlaps with Mr. Ohno's concept of the Toyota production system.

> The factory workers asked me to build an 800-square-yard warehouse. When I asked what they planned to store there, they said, "This part and that part." Since only the subcontractors used these parts, I persuaded them to send all finished parts to the subcontractor, eliminating our need for a warehouse.
>
> Some time later, they came to me again, requesting to buy a new piece of equipment. They complained that since they had no money, they couldn't afford to buy it even if they wanted to. I told them that timing the process differently would eliminate the piles of 20 or 30 parts next to the process, allowing one machine to do the work. With this change, ¥200 million could be raised in no time. It was a matter of using time efficiently. After all, time is valuable.[5]

▸ The insanity that fosters entrepreneurial spirit is a source of human creativity

Henry Ford's invention of the Model T automobile and Mr. Honda's of the Super Cub motorcycle seemed to be the result of a type of insanity in terms of human thinking conditions — an insanity that, in fact, may be common among artists. Similar to the artist mentality is the entrepreneurial spirit that generates modern technological innovation. I think this "insanity" can frequently intensify our creative energy and serve as a trigger for an immense explosion.

We can detect this insanity in Kyocera's Inamori Kazuo's thinking and behavior. Born in 1932, a generation after Mr. Honda, Mr. Inamori himself admits this.

> When I think about my various strong aspirations, they make absolutely no sense. Strong aspirations refer to desires in my heart. Aspirations that penetrate my subconscious are particularly powerful. I feel insanity is responsible for development. As for development and implementation, unless one is crazy, it is impossible to be creative. People who can think only within the bounds of common sense cannot be creative.[6]

By thinking things over repeatedly like a lunatic, aspirations will penetrate the subconscious. Mr. Inamori believes that when this happens, we will be able to travel back and forth between reality and the ideal world without realizing it. Let's look at a concrete example.

> In the beginning I can't tell whether my dreams are dreams or illusions. Gradually, the gap between my dreams and reality shrinks and my dreams emerge when I do crazy things. For example, take the jewelry business. It's said that jewelry businesses fail 99 percent of the time. Everyone warned me, but while busy contemplating various things, I developed the absolute confidence that I could do it and succeed. Today, nobody believes my business will fail. It seems that all of us are mentally deranged. All of us believe we will definitely succeed.[7]

Insanity refers to extreme mental concentration, a single-minded obsession with a certain object. Insanity enables us to see what we normally cannot see.

Can you generate insanity and control it?

Professor Iwai Kan, an authority on psychiatry, comments on the link between human insanity and imagination in his book *Insanity As Humanism*:

> First, insanity provides us with the opportunity to experience things that transcend the normal world, namely things that cannot be experienced under normal conditions. Secondly, insanity has the characteristic of rising above normalcy. Similarly, any genius can transcend normalcy. However, the directions differ. Sometimes the two merge, stimulating our creative energy. Thirdly, the bitterness of insanity deepens the human spirit, and this deepening can be connected to creativity.[8]

Although there is the possibility that insanity is related to imagination, it is remote. Professor Iwai warns us that insanity alone is not responsible for the realization of creativity. In other words:

> Insanity transcends normalcy. However, insanity itself is not related to creativity but to the human subject who possesses the insanity. Therefore, if the human subject cannot control his or her insanity, or is manipulated by that insanity, insanity and imagination become completely unrelated. Consequently, without a balance between the insanity and the strength to control, examine, and capture it, the strength of imagination will also weaken.[9]

The term "genius" refers to creative minorities such as Albert Einstein and Pablo Picasso. However, possessors of the entrepreneurial spirit and creators of modern innovation are also geniuses. But there must be more to it. The robust entrepreneurial spirit in today's industries must design a creative majority.

▸ America's leaders have begun to practice "Management By Wandering Around" (MBWA)

Tom Peters criticizes American managers for not breathing the air of the workplace. He scrupulously instructs them how to recognize the needs of customers by standing in the marketplace. He blames the term "management," with its closed, authoritative, and bureaucratic connotations and explains the need to incorporate a less restricted leadership.

> That last, the concept of leadership, is crucial to the revolution now under way — so crucial that we believe the words "managing" and "management" should be discarded. "Management," with its attendant images — cop, referee, devil's advocate, dispassionate analyst, naysayer, pronouncer — connotes controlling and arranging and demeaning and reducing. "Leadership" connotes unleashing energy, building, freeing, and growing.[10]

The Japanese term for "management" is *kanri*. As if to prove the accuracy of the translation, it, too, connotes "control." The fact that one of America's top management consultants plainly casts away management in favor of leadership illustrates the decline of traditional American management. Mr. Peters advocates "Managing By Wandering Around" (MBWA) as the most appropriate weapon for overcoming this problem.

> And leadership *can* be adaptive, too. The brand we propose has a simple base of MBWA (Managing By Wandering Around). To "wander," with customers (at least 25 percent of the time) and vendors and our own people, *is* to be in touch with the first vibrations of the new. It turns out that hard-data-driven information is usually a day late and *always* sterile.[11]

It is possible to hire specialists to organize and analyze the massive amounts of information absorbed from the company and the outer business world if we choose to plant ourselves in our magnificent city offices. Through the fusion of computers and communications facilities, personal computers, and the far-reaching information network, it presently seems possible to provide the needed goods in the needed amounts at the needed time. However, in reality, as Mr. Peters indicates, such information is based on hard data, which is past information. Soft data is human information. Every customer has a different personality and different preferences, a different scent we should track down. This is what Mr. Peters calls raw data or true information. In the same manner, managers should stand in the production workplace and carefully examine the expressions and feel the attitudes of the employees actually making the products. Only with enthusiastic activity and close teamwork will we be able to make a product that will be well-received by the consumer.

The strength of Japanese management, both in the case of the Toyota production system and TQC, is workplace management. Although they have a production-plant bias, Japanese managers have come to understand the value of both the production workplace as well as the marketplace. Yet the workplace management of Japanese managers still needs polishing. Only when American management attains the standards desired by Tom Peters will American management be reborn.

▸ Henry Ford says entrepreneurs must set standards for the public's sake

When reviewing the life of Henry Ford, we cannot help but notice the amazing business results generated by the industrial and social revolutions symbolized by the Model T. In sharp contrast, we are struck by his anti-labor and anti-Semitic attitudes. Conspicuously, his self-righteous management, which prevented him from trusting his sons and grandchildren, alienated him also from his faithful and talented associates. We can praise and criticize him. However, in any case, his contribution to twentieth-century industrial history is indisputable.

Henry Ford's entrepreneurial spirit enabled him to make paths where none existed. Charles E. Sorensen, his associate and right-hand man, wrote *My Forty Years with Ford* in which he conveys the true essence of the Ford managerial revolution.

In 1914, Henry Ford launched the revolutionary five-dollar daily wage. This was the start of modern industrial production as well as the beginning of new complications between worker and machine. It also marked the birth of modern management, which would create harmony between worker and machine and generate innovation for the new age.

> In March, 1956, the minimum wage became by act of Congress $1 an hour or $8 a day. Back in 1914, Henry Ford raised *his* minimum wage from $2 to $5 a day. The passage of time has dulled the significance and far-reaching results of that action of more than 40 years ago. Proportionately, the Ford increase would be equivalent to raising today's $8 a day to $20. But establishment of a $20 minimum wage, fantastic though it seems, would scarcely parallel the Ford announcement either in importance or in world-wide sensation.
>
> The $5 day did not come about by any legislative act. It was not the outcome of collective bargaining. It did not result from any labor pressure — in fact, its establishment without union participation would be illegal today, and the man who made it could be hauled into court for unfair labor practice. The $5 was merely one man's decision, after seeing some chalked figures on a blackboard in his office, that it would be a good business move. And he was entirely unaware that the consequences of that decision would be a revolution in business outlook and economic thought, and the evolution of what today is the distinctly American productive system of free enterprise.
>
> The Model T was built so that every man could run it. Ford mass production made it available to everyone. Ford wages enabled everyone to afford it. The Ford $5 day rejected the old theory

that labor, like other commodities, must be bought in the cheapest market. It recognized that mass producers are also mass consumers, that they cannot consume unless they are able to buy. But, like Ford mass production, the principles of Ford wages were not expressed until years after the event.

In a recent advertisement was a photograph of Memorial Gate at the University of Pennsylvania. Over it was a Latin inscription of which the English translation is, "We shall find a way or we shall make one." That was also the working philosophy of Henry Ford in the days of his greatness and when he arrived at the $5-day plan.[12]

A $5 daily wage will enhance worker motivation

Many stories exist concerning the Sunday morning meeting at which the $5 daily wages were set. Mr. Sorensen confidently writes:

> I am the only man alive who took part in that meeting; and since none of the others ever set down their accounts, mine is the only first-hand recollection.[13]

Even biographies, which should be trustworthy, should be written with some modesty. Mr. Sorensen's personality and biases appear in his. Let's believe his depiction of this historically critical moment. The four men present at the meeting were Henry Ford; Ed Martin, his production maintenance supervisor and foreman; John Lee, his personnel manager; and Charles Sorensen.

> Mr. Ford had a blackboard in his office. On it I chalked up figures for materials, overhead, and labor based on expanding production and lowered car prices. As expected, production rose, costs fell, and up went figures for profits. Mr. Ford then had me transfer figures from profits column to labor costs — $2 million, $3 million, $4 million. With that daily wage, figures rose from minimums of $2 to $2.50 and $3. Ed Martin protested. I began to see how the increases would give greater incentive to our workers and that savings from lower costs and resulting higher production might be sufficient to take care of the major part of the increases. I could envisage more efficient production facilities that would re-

duce cost, and that there would be further economies from satisfied, willing workers.

While I stood at the blackboard, John Lee commented upon every entry and soon became pretty nasty. It was plain he wasn't trying to understand the idea and thought he might sabotage it by ridiculing it. This didn't set well with Mr. Ford, who kept telling me to put more figures down — $3.50, $3.75, $4.00, $4.25, and a quarter of a dollar more, then another quarter.

At the end of about four hours, Mr. Ford stepped up to the blackboard. "Stop!" he said. "Stop it, Charlie; it's all settled. Five dollars a day minimum pay and at once."[14]

The $5 daily wage was Henry Ford's greatest standard. As a son of the managerial revolution, he naturally was treated as a heretic. Mr. Sorensen explains the level of common sense among managers in 1914

When the entrepreneurial spirit overlaps with creative destruction, heresy approaches legitimacy. The eternal nature of the entrepreneurial spirit is nothing but the spirit of facing legitimacy and being legitimate, while not being limited by it.

Until then, American business had operated on the principle that prices should be kept at the highest point at which people would buy. That is still the operating principle of much French and British industry. But the foundation of the American industrial system, which today outproduces the world, is the mass production technique worked out at Ford Motor Company coupled with Henry Ford's economic heresies that higher wages and lower prices resulted in more abundant production at lower cost.[15]

▸ Don't confuse the purpose with the means!

Henry Ford continued to set his own management standards. This excerpt from his book *Today and Tomorrow* describes his fundamental concepts.

One has to go rather slowly on fixing standards, for it is considerably easier to fix a wrong standard than a right one. There is the standardizing which marks inertia, and the standardizing which marks progress. Therein lies the danger in loosely talking about standardization.

There are two points of view — the producer's and the consumer's. Suppose, for instance, a committee or a department of the government examined each section of industry to discover how many styles and varieties of the same thing were being produced, and then eliminated what they believed to be useless duplication and set up what might be called standards. Would the public benefit? Not in the least — excepting in war time, when the whole nation has to be considered as a productive unit. In the first place, no body of men could possibly have the knowledge to set up standards, for that knowledge must come from the inside of each manufacturing unit and not at all from the outside. In the second place, presuming that they did have the knowledge, then those standards, although perhaps effecting a transient economy, would in the end bar progress, because manufacturers would be satisfied to make to the standards instead of making to the public, and human dignity would be dulled instead of sharpened.[16]

▼

Mito's Commentary B

▸ TQC's strength lies in human operations that always pursue totality and limitlessness

The word "total" in total quality control (TQC) has a relative meaning. In Asian terms, it implies limitlessness.

When secondary manufacturing industries implement TQC, the term implies the total concepts and implementation of quality control and cost reduction as well as the development of new products and techniques. Of course, this is in the production workplace, as well as in headquarters and all indirectly related departments, such as research and development or accounting.

TQC, a uniquely Japanese management technique, is an effective means for corporations to set and accomplish goals within a given time period. On one hand, top management must exert strong and persuasive leadership. On the other, small group activities are used creatively to develop pleasant working environments and realize improved quality and cost reduction. TQC's real merit can be exerted fully through the interaction between such top-down and bottom-up activities.

American-style quality control (QC) methods specifically targeted the production plant. Japanese QC is unique in the respect that it is applied to the production area in a holistic manner, expanding the sphere of humane QC circle activities and striving for totality. This is why QC is referred to as distinctly Japanese.

I feel the most salient characteristic and merit of this uniquely Japanese TQC is its people-centered approach. Nishihori Eizaburo (1904–) explains this simply with humor in his book *Rules for Quality Control*. He writes that the key to quality control is "human" quality control.

> When analyzing quality control in Nishihori-style TQC, the basis for the most serious problems lies in workerpower. These difficulties are closely related to the treatment or management of employees. In other words, from the time I first started implementing QC, I realized workerpower was the key to solving and improving hard quality problems and deepening trust. No matter how machines may take over production through automation, workers ultimately will be responsible for production. To implement QC successfully, therefore, workerpower maintenance, or human quality control, is necessary.[17]

He seems to be stating the obvious, but implementing the obvious *is* difficult. A surprising number of managers tend to focus on "hard" quality, and ignore human quality. Nishihori-style TQC reads the Chinese characters for "human quality" as *jinshitsu* instead of *hitojichi* (hostage). If we read them as the latter, it would be better to interpret the relationship between it and TQC as workers taking the president hostage in order to create a better working environment — instead of the president taking workers hostage to implement hard quality control.

In reality, TQC's success depends on the president's resolution to assume 100-percent responsibility. W. Edwards Deming, on the subject of TQC management by Japanese corporations, once commented, "Eight-five percent of TQC's success depends on the president." The president should imagine him or herself taken hostage by TQC and become devoted to human quality control, even if it means cancelling numerous evening social engagements.

TQC originated from American-style QC techniques developed in 1926 by Dr. Deming's mentor, Walter A. Shewhart of Bell Laboratories. With the arrival of Dr. Deming in 1946, and under his fervent instruction, these QC techniques were disseminated throughout Japan. Later, with J. M. Duran's frequent visits, the effectiveness of statistical quality control (SQC) became known among Japanese corporations. TQC continues to stimulate Japanese innovation and has become firmly established as Japanese management's most effective technique. It is in the process of being exported abroad.

The Deming Prize stimulates corporations to implement and master TQC. The Japan Quality Control Award has been established to push the goal of the Deming Prize even further. It alludes to the limitlessness of TQC. Looking back at its award-winning history, Toyota accepted the Deming Application Prize in 1965 and the Japan Quality Control Award in 1970. Moreover, in 1981, President Toyoda Shoichiro was awarded the Deming Prize.[18]

The various companies belonging to the Toyota Group have made amazing progress with TQC. Needless to say, despite its harmony and discord with TQC, implementation of the Toyota production system also has made noteworthy progress.

▸ Japanese companies have developed Japanese-style QC and ZD

By the late 1960s, following quality control's implementation, the zero defects (ZD) movement had been imported already from the United States and was spreading quickly among Japanese companies.

ZD was a production technique and management routine developed in 1962 by Martin Company [today's Martin Marietta], an aerospace and technology company. It was conceived by them during a crisis for a project that had to be completed at all costs. Indeed, necessity is the mother of all invention and development.

The delivery period for most Defense Department missiles is two months from the order date. However, when a state of emergency required the military to demand that the delivery period be shortened to two weeks, the people involved in missile production discussed how to meet this deadline in each stage of the production process. It was clearly impossible unless they could make a perfect missile the very first time without the tests and readjustments that normally follow final assembly. In other words, they would have to achieve a defect-free product throughout every production stage.

Eliminating the smallest defects at each process stage — from design errors to parts defects to wiring mistakes to final assembly problems — was expected to be extremely difficult. However, the employees and organization had no choice but to succeed. The company successfully met the two-week delivery deadline.

American-style ZD first was introduced to Japan in 1965 through Nihon Electric where it evolved in a uniquely Japanese manner. From the late 1940s, QC concepts from the United States had been implemented aggressively in Japan where companies actively began developing their own QC circle activities. Nihon Electric had also adopted QC activities early on. With the introduction of the ZD movement, it established Nihon Electric ZD management, which was dependent on total employee involvement. Structurally, it was based on QC's small group activities and the small groups were called ZD groups. The ZD movement was promoted in all departments, regardless of type of operation, and has become the company's source of corporate and international competitive power.

In his book *The Original ZD Program,*[19] J. F. Halpern comments that Martin's original intention was to make ZD a plan that motivated workers to do their jobs correctly. Furthermore, in a book on Nihon Electric,[20] he explains that the ZD movement removes the source of errors by doing the job correctly and working efficiently in terms of quality, cost, and delivery through the care and innovation of every employee.

The Japan Productivity Association has been the main organization promoting ZD implementation and incorporation. On the other hand, the Japanese Union of Scientists and Engineers (JUSE) (*Nikka Giren*) promoted QC as conceived by American professors Shewhart and Deming and enabled it to develop into a Japanese-style TQC.

▸ The NPS Research Association is searching for a management system viable in the new Information Age based on the fundamentals of the Toyota production system

NPS stands for "New Production System." It strives to combine the elimination of all production waste and management waste arising from both within the company and outside. Only a formidable organization will pursue such ambitious ideals and utilize the wisdom and efforts of other thoughtful and active people.

The NPS Research Association was founded in 1982[21] under its parent body, the MIP Corporation, and a working capital of ¥1.27 billion ($5.78 million). MIP stands for "Mutual Identity and Prosperity." Co-founder and President Kinoshita Mikiya was formerly president of Ushio Electric.

Association members are listed in Table 4. At the time of its founding, two core members were Tosei Ichiro, the president of Oiresu Kogyo, and Horo Shojin, the president of Kibun. Mr. Kinoshita's mission was to implement management that totally eliminated waste. His enthusiasm for the pursuit of real management — rare in Japan — stimulated original members to make visible progress.

That such production and management concepts would match Mr. Ohno and Suzumura Kikuo's view of management and life is not surprising. Mr. Ohno is the ex-vice president of Toyota while Mr. Suzumura is ex-director of Toyota's production maintenance department who rightfully inherited

MIP Co., Ltd. (Capital: ¥127 million); President: Mikiya Kinoshita; Address: Ichikawa Building, 5-13-3 Ginza, Chuo-ku, Tokyo; Telephone: 03 (545) 1851						
Date of Membership	**Company**	**Representative**	**Capital** *(millions of yen)*	**Sales** *(millions of yen)*	**Employees**	**Main Line of Business**
January 1981	Oiresu	Seiichiro Azuma	450	20,200	665	Oil-less bearings
January 1981	Kibun	Masahito Hoashi	692	192,000	4,200	Fish-paste products
January 1981	Ogura Hoseki Seiki	Koozaburo Ogura	50	3,000	310	Industrial jewels, acoustic products
January 1981	Ikuyo	Masayoshi Sakai	100	11,000	350	Rubber, synthetic resin products
January 1981	Yoga Seiko	Osamu Hisayama	1,000	1,200	105	Telecommunication equipment
March 1981	Shinshin Shokuryo	Maki Kagoshima	160	19,000	350	Food products
April 1981	• Yokogawa Hokushin Electric	Shozo Yokogawa	11,357	139,000	5,500	Industrial instruments
December 1981	• Skylark	Tasuku Chino	1,425	72,805	2,211	Family restaurants
April 1982	Ishikawa Gasket	Itsuo Ishikawa	200	5,550	270	Automotive parts
April 1982	Nippon Atsudenki	Fuminori Sato	210	10,000	450	Electrical acoustic products, wireless equipment
September 1982	Hokusei Aluminum	Takeo Sato	1,000	26,000	625	Light metal casting and rolling
December 1982	• Ihara Koatsu Tsugite	Tsutomu Ihara	500	9,000	383	Couplings, valves
December 1982	• Nipponcoinco	Masaharu Okada	3,027	12,500	320	Coin-operated mechanisms
January 1983	Asia Securities Printing	Morio Ueno	4,800	1,600	120	Financial printing
January 1983	Showa Denki Kogyo	Michio Ura	160	16,000	560	Design and building of electrical installations
January 1983	• Kawasaki Electric	Noboru Kawasaki	640	10,100	416	Electrical equipment (mainly switchboards)
January 1983	Hokusei Nikkei Katei Yohin	Kenzo Kasama	400	10,000	372	Aluminum household goods

Date of Membership	Company	Representative	Capital (millions of yen)	Sales (millions of yen)	Employees	Main Line of Business
June 1983	• Okamoto Machine Tool Works	Taizo Hosoda	3,049	17,200	520	Machine tools, grinding machines
October 1983	• Nozawa	Taichiro Nozawa	1,000	16,200	618	Corrugated slates, boards
November 1983	World	Hirotoshi Hatasaki	920	120,700	2,163	Women's, men's, and children's apparel
January 1984	• Nippon Light Metal	Hosuke Asano	25,300	279,800	4,874	Aluminum smelting, light pressed goods
May 1984	Showa Maruto	Isao Sato	50	12,500	66	Paper tubes for magnetic tapes
September 1984	• Misawa Homes	Chiyoji Misawa	4,397	126,200	1,158	Prefabricated homes
October 1984	• Bando Chemical Industries	Shigeo Ichiki	3,700	48,000	2,015	Belts and industrial goods
February 1985	Asahi Tokushu Gohan	Torakazu Kaibori	550	12,600	473	Plywood
February 1985	• Shizuki Denki Seisakusho	Kiyokazu Ootsu	1,817	12,100	220	Film capacitors
May 1985	• Hokuetsu Kogyo	Masao Ishida	1,001	23,000	660	Air compressors
May 1985	Nippon Filing	Enpei Tajima	35	11,100	520	Steel cabinets and other storage systems
February 1986	• Noritsu	Toshiro Ohta	5,460	60,500	1,585	Gas furnaces, hot water equipment
February 1986	Kurinappu	Noboru Inoue	1,635	51,000	1,929	Bathroom cabinets, kitchen cabinets
February 1986	• Shintokogio	Yuzuru Nakai	2,618	28,900	993	Foundry plant
February 1986	Supankurito Seizo	Yoshihiro Murayama	230	3,000	140	Secondary concrete products
May 1986	• Uni Charm	Keiichiro Takahara	2,312	82,000	476	Paper diapers, sanitary products
May 1986	Shin Nikkei	Shohei Kawakami	3,000	143,500	2,157	Aluminum sash

(Listed in order of admission to membership. Bullets denote companies listed on the Tokyo Stock Exchange or a local stock exchange or trading over-the-counter.)

Table 4. Member Companies of the NPS Research Association

[Table taken from Isao Shinohara, *New Production System: JIT Crossing Industry Boundaries* (Cambridge, MA: Productivity Press, 1988).]

Mr. Ohno's ideas. Both men have spent their lives designing and constructing the Toyota production system. NPS and the MIP Corporation have quite a threesome in the form of Mr. Ohno as chief advisor, Mr. Suzumura in charge of implementation, and Mr. Kinoshita in charge of organizational management. We hope they will stimulate unique management innovation in Japan's industrial world. We further anticipate they will devise a living model of a farsighted management style that will pierce the mature economy.

Applications for membership to the NPS Research Association are pouring in. However, there are a limited number of instructors for implementation and under Suzumura Kikuo's leadership, membership probably will remain restricted. Mr. Suzumura, even more than Mr. Ohno, does not permit any relaxation in the world of production and management. He detects the slightest hidden waste in the production workplace, the marketplace, and even the distribution processes. He also has the ability to arrange the parts into a whole. Because NPS is composed of people filled with the kind of insanity already mentioned, they probably will not be distracted by the secular world.

It is obvious why they choose only one corporation from each industry. In this world, there is probably no other multi-industry exchange group with such clear goals of exposing the corporate ego and pursuing true management.

▸ *What is our business?* should not be asked when times are bad, but now, during prosperity, regardless of how difficult this may be — Peter F. Drucker

There are many ways to describe the characteristics of the Toyota production system, ranging from its organization to operation techniques. A brief humanistic definition might be: the ability to be sensitive to injuries and to be expressive about it. In other words, car sales fluctuate. It implies that we must enjoy being attuned to the subtle changes in the marketplace and deal with them accordingly.

The "amount needed" produced by the Toyota production system is based on market demands, namely customer orders. Therefore, if demand falls, the production quantity decreases. If demand rises, production is altered accordingly. The Toyota production system is based on concepts and techniques that eliminate wastes from all types of production workplaces. However, the system is not confined to production but can be applied to management problems extending into other areas. In fact, it has already exhibited its effectiveness as a management system.

Peter F. Drucker, American scholar of business management, has studied many corporations and observed fascinating conflicts. On the basis of his experiences, he comments that most people in top management ask the question, "What is our business?" when times are bad. He states that the question should be asked now when times are good because only top management can determine the company's course and establish its goals. But, he admits, in reality this question is rarely asked.

Managers tend to trigger arguments, counterarguments, and discord. By posing such questions, divisions and disagreements develop within top management itself. People who had worked side by side for years and believed that they understood each other suddenly would realize that their ideas were fundamentally different. They would be shocked.

Management strives for efficiency. By pursuing the overall efficiency of resources such as manpower, goods, money, information, and time, it designs and implements sophisticated strategies to guarantee success in a free marketplace. The more the company succeeds, the larger it becomes. To cope effectively with this growth, it must do things such as set up an accounting system and concentrate on management resources for improving managerial effectiveness.

Upper managers who fail to ask "What is our business?" have forgotten their true responsibility. This is a natural, negative attribute of executives. It is the most serious cause of the bureaucracy that occurs naturally as an organization grows. This is true of companies in both Japan and the West.

Can we eliminate this problem before it spreads? Is there no way to predict it? It is the same in production and management. We must design a device that automatically will stop a machine if it begins to make defective products. This is the autonomation, or automation with a human touch, in the Toyota production system. It would be useful, however, to acquire the habit of asking "What is our business?" when times are prosperous, as Mr. Drucker advises.

▸ Is there a limit to the superiority of Japan's production technology, the driving force behind its international competitiveness in the world economy?

The strength of Japan's competitive economic edge is symbolized by high-quality cars and VCRs, as well as its competitive pricing. TQC and the Toyota production system are the power behind this edge.

For example, as the name indicates, TQC development involves QC circle activities that concern the whole company on all levels — not just in production, but also at headquarters, in the sales department, and in affiliated and cooperating companies. Through employee improvement proposals, QC circle activities strongly encourage self-improvement and innovation in everyone's operations and work areas. This in turn stimulates the desire to participate in the overall corporate planning. Moreover, it attempts to establish a participatory awareness by all employees. In this sense, it is possible to think of Japanese products, renowned for their high quality, as the fruit of this employee awareness. On the other hand, production technology is the ultimate source of the international competitive edge of these products. We should wonder how long this superiority will be able to support the Japanese economy.

Various issues have been raised. One of the most impressive is the opinion of Kichikawa Hiroyuki, an engineering professor at Tokyo University. He has been examining the future of robots and human society. His resulting proposal is both original and constructive.

Great Britain-United States-Japan?

To prove his hypothesis that it is impossible to maintain forever a superiority in production technology, Professor Kichikawa discusses the source of Great Britain's industrial revolution in the latter half of the eighteenth century.

From the eighteenth to the nineteenth century, industrial developments brought the dramatic change from manual work to the machine industry. This resulted in Britain's Golden Age, propelled by its production technology and economy. With this opportunity, the long and mighty history of the British Empire began. The strength of its production technology, however, was not everlasting. With the twentieth century, the United States grabbed the initiative with amazing vigor. The Ford system, characterized by its mass production of the Model T, was overwhelming.

Our attention is drawn by what happened to Britain and the shock of its defeat. After all, the British Empire had secret powers to support its remarkable status. There was the international insurance system, represented by Lloyd's of London, and the international banking system. There was also Reuters news agency, symbol of its international information network. The strength of such "software" supported its weakening "hardware," namely its production technology. During this time, Britain's political strength remained sound.

Having attained supremacy, did the United States enjoy it as long as Britain had? The answer is no. Japan took the lead from the United States in the late twentieth century by developing and implementing techniques such as TQC and the Toyota production system.

Did America's strength disappear after this? No. It is true that the steel industry in Pittsburgh and the automobile industry in Detroit showed signs of decline after overstepping the bounds of maturity. President Reagan even grew hoarse shouting "reindustrialization!" Has America's automobile industry recovered? It is unreasonable to expect Lee Iacocca's flashy actions — which saved Chrysler from bankruptcy — to cure everything. However, in the long, dark tunnel of recession, both managers and unions abandoned their complacent attitude, strengthened their determination to make reforms, and started to do so.

As for the U. S. automobile industry, in addition to the sound management of General Motors, Ford, and Chrysler — the Big Three — foreign corporations, especially Japanese automobile companies, have begun on-site production. With the growing intensity of market competition, American automakers probably will develop their inborn entrepreneurial spirit.

The United States had the potential to overwhelm Great Britain's software. Its weapon was computer software, which has already exhibited its strength as a source of power for the "new" American economy. While computer hardware is a Japanese specialty, the United States definitely is more advanced in software. Since true computer superiority is determined by software, we cannot help but be surprised by the source of America's economic strength and the accuracy of its foresight. We also cannot ignore its extraordinary political power, military strength, and international intelligence network.

At this point, I want to comment on the current situation and future of Japan.

How to apply superiority in production technology

From the eighteenth century to the present, Professor Kichikawa illustrates the shift of production technology from Great Britain to the United States to Japan, making objective observations about the superiority and limitations of such technology. He suggests that Japan, presently leading in terms of production technology, should take advantage of its superiority and develop substitute technology and systems in preparation for its inevitable loss of supremacy. He notes:

1. Advanced industrial nations have finished developing. The importance of production technology for development is relatively insignificant.

2. Production technology improves when demand is unlimited. When the demand is limited, however, progress is slow.

3. Production technology is transient. In other words, while superiority is beneficial, once lost, the advantages rapidly disappear.

4. One characteristic of advanced industrial nations is their artificial systemization of the environment. Compared to natural environments, artificial systems environments are unstable.

As long as there are limitations to the superiority of production technology, Japan must plan ahead. Who will take away Japan's supremacy? Whether it will be Korea, Taiwan, Singapore, Malaysia, or some other country is beside the point. It will not be easy for Japan to conceive of and develop substitute technology for the next era. Professor Kichikawa discusses this predicament:

> The technology that will enable Japan to maintain its superiority, outlast production technology, and be profitable after the investment, will not be a new product — it will be a completely new form of technology. Great Britain's insurance system and America's software are good examples. Japan's current possibilities must come from its current technological superiority. Only by doing so will that technology become an original, profitable, uniquely Japanese technology.

The realization of Japan's plans

Mr. Kichikawa's theoretical framework, which envisions the driving force behind a new form of technology, is extremely persuasive.

> Let's look at Japan's situation again. The image that springs to mind is that of an advanced nation with severe spatial limitations, which has constructed manufacturing equipment, buildings, and transportation systems in profusion, and has maintained its high level of productivity. However, one distinct feature is the skillful control of overpopulated artificial environments through the efforts of its people.

> We can conclude, then, that since we already spend almost 10 percent of our gross national product (GNP) on maintaining Japan's overcrowded facilities, naturally we should concentrate on this maintenance problem. At the same time, don't we have the ability to overcome it? Perhaps this ability is still hidden, but there are already visible signs. Our maintenance efforts have reduced the number of railway accidents and perfected the accurate arrival and departure of airplanes. Sophisticated maintenance operations by production workers support nuclear power plants, boasting high rates of operation with periodic inspections, and manufacturing industries, as in electronics with its extremely low defect rates.
>
> A tiny nation with many facilities, Japan has skillfully executed appropriate maintenance operations. Furthermore, by creating a new technological system, namely maintenance technology, as its very own technology, Japan preserves its international supremacy. To devise a system to make this profitable will become a crucial technological step for Japan.

The maintenance funds necessary for social capital (such as production facilities in factories), roads and harbors (service facilities such as city buildings and railways), and various other facilities (such as automobiles and residences for personal use) account for almost 10 percent of the GNP. As for future predictions of this maintenance fee, after high-level economic growth and with an increasingly mature economy, we can expect facilities maintenance and preservation funds to surpass by 50 percent and even 60 percent our social capital investment. *Maintenance technology* currently conjures uninteresting images. However, it is not a mistake to say that it will move into the spotlight in the near future. Professor Kichikawa's specialty is robots that think as well as move, a field he and his colleagues have been working on avidly. These robots will probably play a key role in the future of maintenance technology. At the 1985 arms reduction conference in Geneva, while working on an agreement to ban chemical weapons, Japan's emissary, Imai Takakichi, proposed that the remote surveillance robot system developed by Japan be used for the verification of storage and disuse of chemical substances. It is desirable that Japan's robot system be utilized as peaceful technology even in reducing U. S. and Soviet nuclear arms.

Japan's original goal of "peaceful nation," "peaceful industry," and "peaceful technology" is certainly not bad. It is obvious that Japan's production technology must be built permanently into the corporate structure as a management system. Furthermore, we will be able to proceed to new creative heights in substitute technology and systems in the coming age only when we reembrace this internationally unique plan.

Afterword

I interviewed Taiichi Ohno for the first time exactly ten years ago. At the time, I was deeply impressed by something. I exchanged the following words with Mr. Ohno:

When I commented, "Your father probably named you hoping that you would become a 'patient' child (*ninTAIno*)," he simply replied, "My father named me after his job in Dairen, Manchuria, where he worked with 'firebricks' (*TAIkarenga*)."

I had hoped — and expected — to hear some of Mr. Ohno's unique anecdotes on the topic of patience. This was because I thought of the Toyota production system itself as the fruit of Mr. Ohno's patience over the last 50 years. However, when Mr. Ohno said "firebrick," I was thrown off track.

Until this point, Mr. Ohno's tone had been somewhat indifferent. When walking around the production plant, we noticed waste arising from overproduction and transporting, waste created by unnecessary inventory and movement. He explained that the Toyota production system was a system to eliminate such waste totally. He remarked that the conventional assembly-line mass production system, the Ford system, was the chief instigator of such waste. Unless we leveled production by flattening the mountains and filling in the valleys caused by such waste, we would never eliminate defects. With concepts completely opposing existing ones, we must make every product match different consumer preferences. This forms the base of the Toyota production system. . . .

I cannot remember whether our first interview covered all this, but in any case, he did describe the various types of waste in detail. He explained simple things such as: *to eliminate defects, standard operations must be written and posted where everyone can see them.*

As the interview progressed, Mr. Ohno continued to state the obvious and I began growing irritated, wondering when he would ever get to the main issue. I had come with the intention of having him unravel the complexity of the mechanism and actual applications of the Toyota production system. However, Mr. Ohno presented no difficult words or arguments. I was at a loss what to do.

Thus, from the very first interview I recognized that Mr. Ohno liked to state the obvious. After several interviews, I keenly felt that no other person could state the obvious in such a way as to make one think about things so deeply.

I wonder why. Perhaps this is because Mr. Ohno immediately puts every spontaneous idea to the test. Whether listening to people or watching them, observing animals and plants, picking up a book, enjoying golf or mah-jongg, he takes interest in the ordinary. Everything deeply enters his consciousness to be detonated by contact and freshly interpreted.

For example, let's say we encounter the Japanese characters for bean curd *tōfu* and fermented soybeans *nattō*. Focusing on these two terms imaginatively, we come up with a question. *Nattō* is made from rotten beans. *Tōfu* is composed of processed beans shaped like a block. Were they reversed somewhere along the way?

Mr. Ohno would investigate further. "If *nattō* was written 'rotten beans,' nobody would want to eat it. However, if *tōfu* was written 'rotten beans,' nobody would imagine it to be rotten because it is so white and pretty. Therefore, the characters have been reversed." Devising such an interpretation made Mr. Ohno ecstatic. Although he rarely mentions such episodes, his head is full of them. This is the jewel of Ohno-style "reverse thinking."

What is the source of Mr. Ohno's insight, which is fascinated by the obvious, and perceives and unravels invisible problems? The first thing I noticed was that Mr. Ohno was never biased. Even in the case of the *tōfu* and *nattō*, we cannot solve the problem while full of preconceived notions. Later I realized how inflexible my expectations had been when I was first so disillusioned about the source of his name.

Had I no preconceived notions about Mr. Ohno's name, I would have been able to accept honestly his unpredictable reply of firebricks. At the time, I was unable to even reply, "Firebricks... now, that's interesting." Instead I terminated the conversation consequently missing Mr. Ohno's first-rate story about the "uncommon common."

In reality, in Mr. Ohno's imagination, even inanimate objects such as firebricks become animate. Amazingly, gradually we can see the brick enduring the fire through the combination of the expertise of the people making the bricks and contrasting scientific factors such the selection of materials, processing methods, temperature, and time. Mr. Ohno's life principle for work is: "Approach the true essence of things by doing the obvious as the obvious."

The Toyota production system is no longer a mere production system, but a management system that creates a lively organization. Yet the half century during which Mr. Ohno designed and constructed this system consisted of days of creativity in which he laid each brick, one by one, always creatively destroying his ideal overall structure.

As the war and occupation passed, Japan's economic revival occurred. The era of high-level economic growth continued, led by Japan. This was followed by the "dollar shock," the economic shock in the aftermath of America's stoppage of dollar-gold conversion, and the oil crisis. While shifting to a free economy structure, we were shaken by the diversity of values and preferences in the mature society. The economic friction between Japan and the United States and Japan and Western Europe worsens each day. Both domestic and foreign demands caused by the strong yen continue. The "soft" economy progresses. Facing the twenty-first century, we are entering a new sophisticated information society based on the amalgamation of computers and communications.

The true strength of the Toyota production system lies in its vitality and ability to survive this era and exert its intrinsic value as we proceed towards the new sophisticated information society. It embodies Mr. Ohno's firm and yet flexible spirit.

In this book, Mr. Ohno, the biological and adoptive parent of the Toyota production system, puts his heart and soul into telling the story of its past growth, future plans, and untapped possibilities, ranging from general ideas to concrete implementation details.

Management's leader for the twenty-first century has not been determined yet. One will probably not even be easily developed in the 1990s. This implies that time is becoming denser with the steady advances in technological innovation. This book looks towards the 1990s and suggests a clue to arrive there. We believe that thinking jointly with managers and supervisors climbing the stairs to competitive survival in the 1990s will bring information that will stimulate our imagination.

It goes without saying that we need not only to offer products, or hardware, but also to include information, or software, in dealing with the theme of the time — to provide needed goods at the needed time in the needed quantities. In the spirit of two-way communication, we hope you will send us your honest criticisms and comments.

Setsuo Mito
February 1986

Notes

Chapter 1

1. From "My Resume," a series in the *Japan Economic Journal* from September 18, 1985 to October 15, 1985.
2. Charles E. Sorensen with Samuel T. Williamson, *My Forty Years at Ford* (New York: W.W. Norton & Company, 1956), 117–118.
3. Taiichi Ohno, *Toyota Production System: Beyond Large-Scale Production* (Cambridge, Massachusetts: Productivity Press, 1988), 77.
4. Ibid., 87.
5. Ibid., 7–8.
6. Itoh Masatoshi, *Business Considerations* (Tokyo: Kodansha, 1984).

Chapter 2

1. Henry Ford with Samuel Crowther, *Today and Tomorrow* (Garden City, NY: Doubleday, Page & Company, 1926), 108–109. [Long out of print, this book is currently available in a 1988 anniversary reprint edition from Productivity Press.]
2. Ibid., 109.
3. Ibid., 110.
4. Alfred P. Sloan, *My Forty Years with General Motors* (Garden City, NY: Doubleday, 1964).
5. Daniel J. Boorstin, *The Americans: The Democratic Experience* (New York: Vintage Books, 1974), 552.
6. Max Picard, *Die Welt des Schweigens*, (Erlenbach-Zurich: E. Reutsch, 1959). Published in German in 1948 and translated into English in 1952.
7. Taiichi Ohno, op. cit., 48–49.

Chapter 3

1. Thomas J. Peters and Nancy K. Austin, *A Passion for Excellence: The Leadership Difference* (New York: Random House, 1985).
2. Thomas J. Peters and Robert H. Waterman, *In Search of Excellence* (New York: Harper & Row, 1982).
3. Honda Soichiro, *Living on Speed* (Jitsugyo no Nihonsha, 1954).
4. Honda Soichiro, *Zakkubaran* (Jidosha Weekly Co., 1960).
5. Ibid.
6. Inamori Kazuo, *Kyocera's Philosophy* (Vol. 5, February 1977).
7. Ibid.
8. Iwai Kan, *Insanity as Humanism* (Japan Broadcasting Publishing Co., 1981).
9. Ibid.
10. Peters and Austin, op. cit., xvii.
11. Ibid., 7.
12. Charles E. Sorensen, op. cit., 135–136.
13. Ibid., 137.
14. Ibid., 139.
15. Ibid., 144.
16. Henry Ford, op. cit., 78.
17. Nishihori Eizaburo, *Hinshitsu kanri kokoroecho* (Rules of Quality Control) (Japan Standards Association, 1981).
18. The Deming Prize was established in Japan in 1950 by the Union of Japanese Scientists and Engineers (JUSE) with proceeds from reprints of Dr. Deming's lectures donated to Japan's quality effort. Awarded yearly, the prize is actually several: the Deming Prize for individuals and the Deming Application Prize with subcategories for large and small companies, divisions, and plants. [Mary Walton, *The Deming Management Method* (New York: Dodd, Mead & Company, 1986), 122.]
19. J. F. Halpern, *Gentei ZD Program* (The Original ZD Program) (Japan Productivity Association, 1968).
20. J. F. Halpern, *ZD no jissai* (The Truth about ZD) (Japan Productivity Association, 1966).
21. For a study in English of this organization, refer to: Isao Shinohara, *New Production System: JIT Crossing Industry Boundaries* (Cambridge, Massachusetts: Productivity Press, 1988).

About the Authors

Taiichi Ohno

Taiichi Ohno was born in Dairen (Port Arthur), Manchuria, China, in February, 1912. In 1932, after graduating from the department of mechanical engineering, Nagoya Technical High School, he joined Toyoda Spinning and Weaving. In 1943, he was transferred to the Toyota Motor Company where he was named machine shop manager in 1949. He became Toyota's director in 1954, managing director in 1964, senior managing director in 1970, and executive vice president in 1975. Although he retired from Toyota in 1978, Mr. Ohno continues as chairman of Toyoda Spinning and Weaving. He resides in Toyota-shi, Aichi-ken.

This book first appeared in Japan in May, 1978, and reached its 20th printing in February, 1980. Productivity Press's 1988 edition is the first printed for the English-reading public.

Other books available in English by Mr. Ohno are *Toyota Production System: Beyond Large-Scale Production* (1988) and *Workplace Management* (1988).

Setsuo Mito

Setsuo Mito was born in 1934 in Horishima Prefecture. He was graduated in 1959 by Keio University's School of Law. As an economics journalist, he worked for the Japanese business magazines *Shukan Diamond*, from 1959–1964, and *President*, from 1964–1977. In 1977, he became a freelance reporter and a newscaster for Japan's national television station, Channel 10.

Besides *Just-in-Time for Today and Tomorrow*, Mr. Mito has written *Honda Management System* and *Revolution in Ceramics*, currently available only in Japanese.

Index

Also from Productivity Press

Productivity Press publishes and distributes materials in the field of quality and productivity improvement for business and industry, the general trade market, and academia. With a special emphasis on improvement systems developed in Japan, these books provide original source materials from recognized authorities in the field — among them Taiichi Ohno. Other products and services from Productivity include conferences and seminars, newsletters, training programs, and industrial study missions to Japan. Call or write for a free catalog.

Toyota Production System
Beyond Large-Scale Production

by Taiichi Ohno

Here's the original — the first information ever published in Japan on the Toyota Production System (also known as Just-In-Time manufacturing), and by the very person who created it for Toyota. In this book you will learn about the origins and development of the system, as well as its underlying philosophy. Any company aspiring to be a world class manufacturer must use the concepts developed by Mr. Ohno. This classic is the place to start.
ISBN 0-915299-14-3 / 164 pages / $39.95

Workplace Management

by Taiichi Ohno

An in-depth view of how one of this century's leading industrial thinkers aproaches problem solving and continuous improvement. Gleaned from Ohno's forty years of experimentation and innovation at Toyota Motor Co., this book explains the concepts that Ohno considers to be most important to successful management, with an emphasis on quality. See how JIT moves beyond the factory floor.
ISBN 0-915299-19-4 / 166 pages / $34.95

Today and Tomorrow

by Henry Ford

Ohno's inspiration! Originally published in 1926, this autobiography by the world's most famous automaker has been long out of print. Yet Ford's ideas have never stopped having an impact, and this book provides direct access to the thinking that changed industry forever. Here is the man who doubled wages, cut the price of a car in half, and produced over 2 million units a year. Time has not diminished the progressiveness of his business philosophy, or his profound influence on worldwide industry. You will be enlightened by what you read, and intrigued by the words of this colorful and remarkable man.
ISBN 0-915299-36-4 / 300 pages / $24.95

Kanban and Just-In-Time at Toyota
Management Begins at the Workplace

edited by the Japan Management Association, translated by David J. Lu

Based on seminars developed by Taiichi Ohno and others at Toyota for their major suppliers, this book is the best practical introduction to Just-In-Time available. It explains every aspect of a "pull" system in clear and simple terms — the underlying rationale, how to set up the system and get everyone involved, and how to refine it once it's in place. A groundbreaking and essential tool for companies beginning JIT implementation.
ISBN 0-915299-08-9 / 186 pages / $29.95

Canon Production System
Creative Involvement of the Total Workforce

compiled by the Japan Management Association

A fantastic success story! Canon set a goal to increase productivity by three percent per month — and achieved it. Here is the only book-length case study to show how to combine Japanese management principles and quality improvement techniques into one overall strategy that improves every area of the company on a continual basis. It shows how the major QC tools are applied in a matrix management model, and how the basic tools of JIT work in a non-automotive manufacturing operation.
ISBN 0-915299-06-2 / 232 pages / $36.95

BOOKS AVAILABLE FROM PRODUCTIVITY PRESS

Christopher, William F. **Productivity Measurement Handbook**
ISBN 0-915299-05-4 / 1983 / 680 pages / looseleaf / $137.95

Ford, Henry. **Today and Tomorrow** (originally published 1926)
ISBN 0-915299-36-4 / 1988 / 302 pages / hardcover / $24.95

Fukuda, Ryuji. **Managerial Engineering: Techniques for Improving Quality and Productivity in the Workplace**
ISBN 0-915299-09-7 / 1984 / 206 pages / hardcover / $34.95

Hatakeyama, Yoshio. **Manager Revolution! A Guide to Survival in Today's Changing Workplace**
ISBN 0-915299-10-0 / 1984 / 198 pages / hardcover / $24.95

Japan Management Association and Constance E. Dyer.
Canon Production System: Creative Involvement of the Total Workforce
ISBN 0-915299-06-2 / 1987 / 251 pages / hardcover / $36.95

Japan Management Association. **Kanban and Just-In-Time at Toyota: Management Begins at the Workplace,** Translated by David J. Lu
ISBN 0-915299-08-9 / 1986 / 186 pages / hardcover / $29.95

Karatsu, Hajime. **Tough Words for American Industry**
ISBN 0-915299-25-9 / 1988 / 179 pages / hardcover / $24.95

Karatsu, Hajime. **TQC Wisdom of Japan: Managing for Total Quality Control**
ISBN 0-915299-18-6 / 1988 / 138 pages / hardcover / $29.95

Lu, David J. **Inside Corporate Japan: The Art of Fumble-Free Management**
ISBN 0-915299-16-X / 1987 / 278 pages / hardcover / $24.95

Mizuno, Shigeru (ed.) **Management for Quality Improvement: The 7 New QC Tools**
ISBN 0-915299-29-1 / 1988 / 326 pages / hardcover / $59.95

Ohno, Taiichi. **Toyota Production System: Beyond Large-Scale Production**
ISBN 0-915299-14-3 / 1988 / 176 pages / hardcover / $39.95

Ohno, Taiichi. **Workplace Management**
ISBN 0-915299-19-4 / 1988 / 176 pages / hardcover / $34.95

Ohno, Taiichi and Setsuo Mito. **Just-In-Time for Today and Tomorrow: A Total Management System**
ISBN 0-915299-20-8 / 1988 / 176 pages / hardcover / $34.95

Shingo, Shigeo. **Non-Stock Production: The Shingo System for Continuous Improvement**
ISBN 0-915299-30-5 / 1988 / 480 pages / hardcover / $75.00

Shingo, Shigeo. **A Revolution in Manufacturing: The SMED System,** translated by Andrew P. Dillon
ISBN 0-915299-03-8 / 1985 / 383 pages / hardcover / $65.00

Shingo, Shigeo. **Zero Quality Control: Source Inspection and the Poka-Yoke System,** translated by Andrew P. Dillon
ISBN 0-915299-07-0 / 1986 / 328 pages / hardcover / $65.00

Shingo, Shigeo. **The Sayings of Shigeo Shingo: Key Strategies for Plant Improvement,** translated by Andrew P. Dillon
ISBN 0-915299-15-1 / 1987 / 207 pages / hardcover / $36.95

Shinohara, Isao (ed.) **New Production System: JIT Crossing Industry Boundaries**
ISBN 0-915299-21-6 / 1988 / 218 pages / hardcover / $34.95

AUDIO-VISUAL PROGRAMS

Shingo, Shigeo. **The SMED System,** translated by Andrew P. Dillon
ISBN 0-915299-11-9 / 181 slides / 40 minutes / $749.00
ISBN 0-915299-27-5 / 2 videos / 40 minutes / $749.00

Shingo, Shigeo, **The Poka-Yoke System**, translated by Andrew P. Dillon
ISBN 0-915299-13-5 / 224 slides / 45 minutes / $749.00
ISBN 0-915299-28-3 / 2 videos / 45 minutes / $749.00

FORTHCOMING FROM PRODUCTIVITY PRESS

Japan Human Resources Association. **The Idea Book: Improvement Through Total Employee Involvement**
ISBN 0-915299-22-4 / October 1988 / $39.95 (tent.)

Nakajima, Seiichi. **Introduction to Total Productive Maintenance**
ISBN 0-915299-23-2 / October 1988 / $39.95 (tent.)

Nikkan Kogyo Shimbun. **An Illustrated Guide to Poka-Yoke Devices: Improving Quality Through the Prevention of Defects on the Shop Floor,** with a foreword by Shigeo Shingo
ISBN 0-915299-31-3 / December 1988 / $50.00 (tent.)

Shingo, Shigeo. **Study of Toyota Production System from Industrial Engineering Viewpoint** (revised edition)
ISBN 0-915299-17-8 / December 1988 / $35.00 (tent.)

TO ORDER: Write, phone or fax Productivity Press, Dept. BK, P.O. Box 3007, Cambridge, MA 02140, phone 617/497-5146, fax 617/868-3524. Send check or charge to your credit card (American Express, Visa, MasterCard accepted).

U.S. ORDERS: Add $3 shipping for first book, $1 each additional. CT residents add 7.5% and MA residents 5% sales tax.

FOREIGN ORDERS: Payment must be made in U.S. dollars. For Canadian orders, add $8 shipping for first book, $1 each additional. Orders to other countries are on a proforma basis; please indicate shipping method desired.

NOTE: Prices subject to change without notice.